REFUGEE CHILD

My memories of the
1956 Hungarian Revolution

Bobbie Kalman
Illustrations by Barbara Bedell

Crabtree Publishing Company
www.bobbiekalmanrefugeechild.com
www.crabtreebooks.com

Crabtree Publishing Company

www.crabtreebooks.com

www.bobbiekalmanrefugeechild.com

Library and Archives Canada Cataloguing in Publication

Kalman, Bobbie, 1947-
   Refugee child : my memories of the 1956 Hungarian Revolution /
Bobbie Kalman.

Includes bibliographical references and index.
ISBN 978-0-7787-2760-6.--ISBN 0-7787-2760-2

1. Kalman, Bobbie, 1947- --Childhood and youth--Juvenile literature.
2. Hungary--History--Revolution, 1956--Juvenile literature. 3. Refugee
children--Biography--Juvenile literature. 4. Hungary--History--
Revolution, 1956--Personal narratives--Juvenile literature. I. Title.

DB957.3.K34 2006   j943.905'2092   C2006-902872-9

Library of Congress Cataloging-in-Publication Data

Kalman, Bobbie.
   Refugee child : my memories of the 1956 Hungarian revolution /
Bobbie Kalman ; illustrations by Barbara Bedell.
   p. cm.
   Includes bibliographical references and index.
   ISBN-13: 978-0-7787-2760-6 (trade hardbound)
   ISBN-10: 0-7787-2760-2 (trade hardbound)
   1. Kalman, Bobbie. 2. Hungary--History--Revolution, 1956--
Personal narratives--Juvenile literature. 3. Refugee children--
Hungary--Biography--Juvenile literature. 4. Refugee children--
Austria--Vienna
--Biography--Juvenile literature. 5. Hungary--History--1945-1989
--Juvenile literature.   I. Bedell, Barbara. II. Title.
DB957.3.K35 2006
943.905'2--dc22
[B]
                                                    2006016157

Crabtree Publishing Company

www.crabtreebooks.com   1-800-387-7650

Published in Canada
Crabtree Publishing
616 Welland Ave.
St. Catharines,
Ontario
L2M 5V6

Published in the
United States
Crabtree Publishing
PMB 16A
350 Fifth Ave.
Suite 3308
New York, NY
10118

Published in the
United Kingdom
Crabtree Publishing
White Cross Mills
High Town,
Lancaster
LA1 4XS

Published in
Australia
Crabtree Publishing
386 Mt. Alexander Rd.
Ascot Vale (Melbourne)
VIC 3032

1 2 3 4 5 6 7 8 9 0 Printed in the U.S.A. 5 4 3 2 1 0 9 8 7 6

For my mother, Valerie Kalman,
with all my love and thanks.
Without your help,
this book could not have been written.

In memory of my father,
Imre Kalman.
I now understand, Dad,
and I love you.

With Much Gratitude

There are so many people to thank, that my gratitude could fill a separate book.

First, I thank my husband, Peter Crabtree, for inspiring me to write my story and for holding my hand through this emotional writing journey.

Our mothers are such an important part of who we are, and I feel so grateful for mine. We've worked together on this story, and it's brought me great joy and wonderful memories. Thank you, Mom, for sharing them with me.

I thank my father, Imre Kalman, for encouraging me to dream and for never letting me forget my heritage.

I am thankful that I had my sister Suzie Kalman by my side during the incredible events that took place in our lives. We were there for each other through it all!

I thank my grandparents for giving me so much love in my first nine years of life. You both live in my heart.

I thank my aunts Blanka and Joli for sharing their stories with me. I am especially grateful to my uncle, Dr. Székelyhidi László, for taking photographs of Mosonmagyaróvár for me and for recounting his memories at the hospital that sad day.

I thank the Huber Family, Tante (Aunt) Burgi and Elfi Schmolka, who were, and are again, my family. I thank Marion Schmolka for her help in scanning the family photos for this book.

I thank Tante Rózsi and Onkel (Uncle) Karl Tauer for turning Vienna into a magical fairy tale! Onkel Karl, you encouraged my imagination and fantasies. You are a Prince!

I thank my childhood friend and "sister" Dusek Zsuzsa, who provided me with maps, photographs, and memories.

I thank my aunts Ditti (Elisabeth Girouard) and Manci (Margaret Brissenden) for helping us start our new lives and my many cousins, especially Pat Girouard and Julie Mercer.

I thank my children, Andrea, Marc, Caroline, and Samantha Crabtree, for their encouragement, especially Andrea who is working hard to promote this book, and Samantha, who helped with the cover design and restored the old photos.

My uncle, Dr. Székelyhidi, wishes to thank the doctors and other healthcare workers in Mosonmagyaróvár, who saved many lives on that terrible October day. Among them were Dr. Zsibói, Dr. Vida Ödön, Dr. Blank Tibor, Dr. Modrovich Emil, Dr. Sugár György, Dr. Ódor Béla, Dr. Munka István, Dr. Kiss András, Dr. Kiss József, Dr. Major Jenö, Dr. Grüner György, Meszlényi Sándor, Veress Béla, Pócza Zoltán, Juranovichné, Beleczné, Ani, Pannika, and many others who worked tirelessly to keep people alive.

I thank the Hungarian freedom fighters who risked their lives, and those who died for our country, so that we could have hope!

How can I ever thank the people of Austria, who opened their country and hearts to nearly 200,000 Hungarian refugees? We were a huge burden to such a small country, yet you treated us with the utmost kindness and respect! I'll never forget the compassion you showed us. You replaced our fear with love and helped heal us.

In Loving Memory

This book is a tribute to the memory of Tom Nagy, known as Tamás in the book. It is his story, too. I dedicate it to his parents János and Ica, his wife Gaby, and his children Matthew, David, and Corina. I know Tom would have loved sharing this last great adventure with me. Those were exciting days, weren't they, Tom?

Tom in 1956

Gaby and Tom

Corina, Matthew, David

With fond memories of Onkel Hans Huber, shown here with daughter Elfi. I'll never forget the love and fun you showed us during a time that could have been very difficult. Instead, those weeks were some of the happiest times of our lives. I'll always remember and love our *"Huberpapschi,"* or Huber Daddy, which is what you were to us.

Special Thanks

Many people helped me with this book. First of all, I would like to thank Barbara Bedell for her lovely illustrations, which bring my story to life.

I thank Kelley MacAulay, who wrote the history section and edited the book several times. I thank Larissa Kostoff for the first comprehensive overhaul of my story, as well as Kathy Middleton, Peter Crabtree, and Michael Hodge for their edits.

I thank Crystal Foxton, our photo researcher, who helped me track down some pictures I thought would be impossible to find. We had fun doing the detective work together.

I thank our designers Rose Gowsell, Robert MacGregor, and Kathy Kantor for making the book look great, Arlene Wilson for scanning, Samara Parent for production assistance, and Samantha Crabtree for restoring the old, damaged, family photos.

I thank Francine Jarry, www.rainbowmusic.ca, for permission to use her songs: *Love Heals Everything* on page 138 and *There's Always Another Boat* on page 176. They say what is in my heart.

I thank Kathy Middleton, Andrea Crabtree, Sean Charlebois, Lisa Antonsen, and Melissa Waters for their tireless work in marketing and promoting this book.

I thank Bryan Dawson-Szilagyi, Executive Committee Chairman of the American Hungarian Federation, for his advice, encouragement, and support of this book.

Photographs and Illustrations

Contents

Introduction

The name of my city

I was born in Mosonmagyaróvár, Hungary. When people see this name, they don't attempt to say it. Actually, it's simple to pronounce when you break it down into the three words from which it is made up: Óvár, Magyar, and Moson. The original town, Óvár, is the downtown area today. It was built around a *vár*, or fort. *Magyar* means "Hungarian" in the Hungarian language. Moson is the name of the town that joined Óvár in 1939, to form the city of Mosonmagyaróvár. Try pronouncing it now that you know the three parts: Moson (moh-shon), Magyar (mah-djar), Óvár (oh-vahr). Most people just call our city Magyaróvár. Try that for starters!

Other areas

Our city is made up of other areas, too, besides Moson and Óvár. The village of Lucsony became part of Mosonmagyaróvár, but its name was not added to the name of the city. Károlyliget, where my grandparents lived, is another part. It is across a river, called the Small Lajta. We had to go over a bridge to get there. Károlyliget was less than ten minutes from our apartment, but it was like another world! Óvár was the city, and Károlyliget was the country, with farm animals and homes that had no indoor plumbing.

(above) This is the fort after which Óvár was named. In 1956, it was the Agricultural Academy. My mother worked in the library of the college.
(below) We lived in this building. Our windows are marked with red ovals.

Important location

Mosonmagyaróvár was close to both the Czechoslovakian and Austrian borders. It was about 6 miles (10 km) from Austria. Because of its location, our small city was especially important during the Hungarian Revolution. People from other countries crossed the Austrian border into Hungary and assembled in Magyaróvár. The Soviet tanks that came from Czechoslovakia to help crush the Revolution also passed through there. After the Revolution ended, many refugees traveled to our city before crossing the border into Austria. This map shows Hungary, its neighboring countries, and some important cities.

Budapest is the capital city of Hungary, and Vienna is the capital city of Austria. The road on which I lived connected these two cities. This map shows the neighboring countries as they were called in 1956.

The City Hall was across the street from our home. We could see what was happening there from our window. To the right of City Hall was the tavern where foreigners gathered.

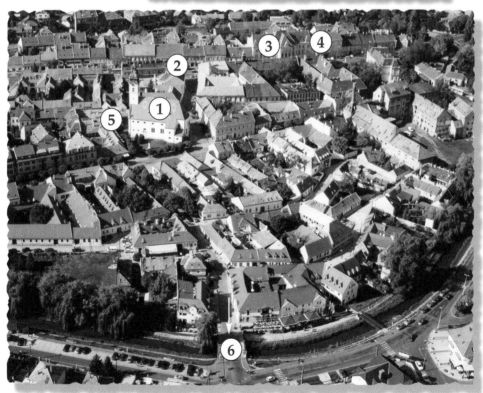

This picture is a view of my city today. I've put numbers on the following: **1.** my church **2.** my home **3.** City Hall **4.** Fekete Sas Tavern **5.** Tamás's house **6.** the bridge to Károlyliget, where my grandparents lived.

A bit about Hungarian names

There are some Hungarian names in this book that may be hard to pronounce. The Hungarian language is not like most other languages. Its alphabet has 42 letters, some with accents, and some which are a combination of letters. Each letter has its own sound, so once you learn the alphabet, you can't make a spelling mistake. However, the pronunciation of Hungarian words is different from that of English words. Below are some Hungarian names that appear in the book, the way they are pronounced, and the English versions of the names:

Hungarian name	Pronunciation	English name
Babi (me)	bubbie	Bobbie
Zsuzsi (my sister)	zhoo-zhie	Suzie
Vali (my mother)	vahl-ee	(short for) Valerie
Imre (my father)	im-reh	Emery
Tamás (my friend)	tom-ahsh	Thomas, Tom
Ica (his mother)	it-sah	Helen
János (his father)	yahn-osh	John
István (Grandpapa)	isht-vahn	Steven
Julia (Grandmama)	yuh-lia	Julia
Blanka (my aunt)	blahn-ka	Blanka
Éva (my aunt)	ava	Eva
Marika (my aunt)	mah-ri-ka	Mary or Maria
Joli (my aunt)	yolie	Yolanda
Laci (short for Lászlo)	laht-zhi	Leslie
László (my uncle Laci)	lahs-low	same as above
Miklós (my uncle)	mick-lowsh	Nicholas

≈ 14 ≈

Hungarian name	Pronunciation	English name
Manci (my aunt)	munt-si	Margaret
Ditti (my aunt)	ditti	Elisabeth
Rózsi (aunt in Vienna and grandmother)	Roh-zhie	Rosie

First and last

In Hungary, your surname, or family name, comes first. For example, my Hungarian name is Kálmán Babi. The name "Kálmán" (kahl-mahn) is my surname. In the book, you may find names written in either order.

Aunts and Uncles that really aren't

The word for "aunt" in Hungarian is *néni*, which is pronounced "neh-nee." The word for uncle is *bácsi*, pronounced "baht-chie." In both Hungary and Austria, "aunt" or "uncle" is added to the name of any adult woman or man, when a child talks to them or about them. It is impolite for a child *not* to add the words. For example, I call my friend's mother "aunt," and I also called some of my real aunts "aunt." Three of my aunts, Blanka, Éva, and Marika, were very young, so I didn't add "aunt" to their names at all. I did, however, use "aunt" to refer to my aunts Joli, Ditti, and Manci.

German words

You may notice that some of the German words included in the book start with capital letters. In the German language, all nouns start with capital letters. Nouns are people, places, and things.

My big family

My mother was born in Magyaróvár. Her parents' names were Vajmár István and Julia. They had seven daughters. From oldest to youngest, they are Ditti, Manci, Vali (my mother), Joli, Blanka, Éva, and Marika. Ditti and Manci left Hungary in 1938 to live in England. There, they met two soldiers from Canada, whom they married. My aunts then immigrated to Canada and had eleven children between them. So far, my grandparents have 68 direct descendants. I am very fortunate to have such a big, wonderful family!

Here are Ditti (left) and Manci, in England. While I lived in Hungary, I'd never met them or my cousins, but I heard many stories about them. They were always a big part of our lives.

From left to right, Aunt Joli, my father, Grandmother Rózsi, (my dad's mother), and my mom. My father was born in Szeged, where his mother and brother lived. (See map on page 12 to see where Szeged is.) I didn't know my father's family well.

(below) My Grandmother Julia is shown here as a young woman.

(below right) The five sisters that lived in Hungary, as children. (back row) my mother, Aunt Joli (front) Éva, Marika, and Blanka

My parents were Kálmán Vali (Valéria) and Imre. My legal name was Mária Valéria, but I've been called Babi, now Bobbie, since birth.

(above) My sister's name was Márta Zsuzsanna. We called her Zsuzsi.
(right) I am five in this picture.

This picture of Zsuzsi (now Suzie) and me was taken in June 1956, on the day of her First Communion. We left Hungary about six months later. My sister was seven years old, and I was almost nine. Zsuzsi has no memories of her childhood in Hungary or of the time we spent in Vienna.

The Nagy family in 1956—Uncle János, Aunt Ica, and my friend Tamás (Tom), who is a big part of my story. Our two families left Hungary together. Tamás was eight when this picture was taken.

My life in Hungary

My life in Hungary was very different from the life of a child living in North America. Although we lived in a large apartment, we had no appliances to help with the housework. There was no washer or dryer or any kind of kitchen appliance, except a gas stove. We had radios, but we had no television sets or telephones. We heated our apartment by burning packed sawdust in ceramic stoves. We were often very cold in winter.

Food and medicine

It was very difficult to get nutritious food in Hungary. People had to line up for hours each day, just to buy a little meat, milk, or bread for their families. My grandparents raised animals, so we didn't starve. They also grew fruit, but I'd never seen fruit such as oranges or bananas before 1956. Medicine was also hard to get. When I was six and my sister was four, we were both hospitalized for over a month with scarlet fever because there were no antibiotics to help us get better. When my friend Tamás got rheumatic fever, he missed a whole year of school.

Communist presence

Letters from outside Hungary were opened and read. When packages arrived from my aunts in Canada, items were missing, but it was still like Christmas! I especially looked forward to getting the Sears catalog. I couldn't believe that people could buy such amazing toys or clothes! The Communists interfered with everything in our lives, but they didn't *always* rain on our parade. They were more like dark clouds that constantly *threatened* rain!

Living under Communist rule

Hungary was occupied by the Soviet Union in 1945, after World War Two. An occupied country is controlled by another country's army. The Soviet Union was a Communist country made up of Russia and several smaller countries. Under Communism, almost all property is owned by the government, and people have to work hard for very little money. Since the Communist government owned almost everything in Hungary, people had no way of making their lives better. It didn't matter how hard my parents worked, we could *never* have become wealthy!

The dreaded ÁVOs!

Hungary was also a police state. In a police state, a secret police force controls the lives of the people. The Hungarian secret police organization was called the ÁVH. The members of the ÁVH were called ÁVOs. If people spoke out against Communism, they were threatened and beaten by the ÁVOs. The ÁVOs also put many people in jail and killed thousands more people. The cruelty of the ÁVOs made us more than just afraid of them. We were terrified!

Locked inside

Many people wanted to leave Hungary, but getting out of the country was almost impossible because there were watchtowers all along Hungary's borders. Soldiers with guard dogs patrolled the borders and killed anyone who tried to cross. In some places, the Soviets even buried landmines that would explode if someone stepped on them. At that time, Hungary was like a huge prison, and none of us could get out—even for a visit.

Radio Free Europe

The Communists wanted to control all the information we received about Hungary and the rest of the world. They banned all non-Communist newspapers and screened all radio broadcasts. We could listen only to radio stations that were approved by the government. But my father and grandfather listened to Radio Free Europe whenever the airwaves weren't blocked by the Communists. They listened in secret. If we overheard them listening to the radio program, we never told a soul. Listening to Radio Free Europe was strictly forbidden! Radio Free Europe was a European radio station funded by the United States. Americans wanted Communist countries to become democracies. In a democracy, people vote for a leader and a government of their choice. They also have a lot of rights and freedoms. Radio Free Europe talked about how much better it was to live in a democratic society.

Who will tell?

We had to watch what we said at all times. There were informants everywhere! Informants were people who told the ÁVOs when anyone spoke out against Communism. Some people were paid to be informants, and some were forced to tell on others. Informants could be co-workers, teachers, friends, or even family members. No one knew who they were, so we had to watch what we said, even in our homes! We felt as though we were being watched at all times, so we couldn't really relax. We learned to keep secrets and tell lies to make sure our families stayed safe. But we wanted to SCREAM out our feelings. We wanted to scream out the truth!

Forget that you're Hungarian!

Communist leaders tried to inject Communist thinking into every part of our lives, including school, the newspapers and radio, and even into our homes. We had to adopt the Soviet culture and Communist beliefs. We learned the Russian language and used Russian textbooks. We had to pretend that we hated our own culture and traditions. We weren't even allowed to sing the Hungarian anthem! And, we couldn't talk about kings or queens or other parts of Hungary's past.

Kalman the Booklover (king from 1095-1116)

One of my favorite Hungarian kings was Könyves Kálmán, or Kalman the Booklover. He was a great king, not only because his name was the same as mine and he loved books like I do, but also because he promoted reading and learning and passed some very important laws. For example, he stopped the burning of witches. He declared that witches did not exist, so there were to be no investigations, no trials, and no burnings. He also made the Holy Crown of Hungary more important than the king who wore the crown. When the country had no king, the territories still belonged to the Crown. The image of the Holy Crown of Hungary is part of the Hungarian coat of arms. (See page 24.)

Flags and coats of arms

At the top of each page in this book, there is a flag or a coat of arms. The Hungarian colors are red, white, and green. Today, the Hungarian flag most often used is plain, with nothing in its center. Sometimes, however, when flags are used for ceremonial purposes, a flag with a Hungarian coat of arms is used.

Hungarian flag

The Hungarian coat of arms

The coat of arms shown below is used on some flags today. I have used it throughout the book. The red and white stripes represent the seven Hungarian tribes, the four white stripes stand for the four main rivers, and the three green hills stand for the three main mountains that, long ago, were part of Hungary. The whole coat of arms is surrounded by branches—an oak branch for "glory" and an olive branch for "peace." At the top rests the Holy Crown of Hungary, also known as the Crown of St. Stephen, the first Hungarian king. No one knows why its cross is bent. Some people feel it was created that way, but others feel that the cross was bent by accident.

Ceremonial flag

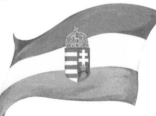

Angels and eagles

An old Hungarian coat of arms, shown left, has two angels, but it is different from the one I used, which is shown right. The one on the left includes the countries that were once part of the Austrian empire long ago.

I thought that I'd created the coat of arms on the right. Imagine my surprise, when my uncle sent me a photo of my old school in Hungary with this *exact* replica of my creation (see page 35)! I used this coat of arms as the symbol of my experiences in Vienna. The center part stands for my Hungarian background, and the angels are the angels I believed were taking care of me while I was in Austria. I also used the double-headed eagle, shown right, which represents the Dual Monarchy of Austria-Hungary. I felt that I was part of both countries.

Torn from the flag

While Hungary was Communist, the Soviet symbol, shown left, dominated the center of the Hungarian flag. The red star, hammer, and wheat stood for the Soviet Union. During the Revolution, the symbol was torn out of the flag to show that Hungarians wanted freedom from Soviet occupation.

Communist flag

Revolutionary flag

Bobbie's Story

Freedom is being able to sing any song you wish
or talk about whatever your heart desires.
Freedom is being able to express
the beauty of who you are
without being punished for it.
Freedom is not having to keep secrets.
Freedom is not being afraid.

Chapter One

A Beautiful Day

It was Friday, October 26, 1956, a sunny day in Magyaróvár. I thought how wonderful it was to have such great weather so late in October. My face felt warm, but I had a cold feeling in my heart. I stood still in front of my apartment building and then walked around the corner to Tamás's house. Tamás was one of my best friends. His parents and mine were best friends, too. Their house was next to the church, about a block away from my building. I rang the doorbell. Tamás's mother answered and kissed me hello.

"Good morning, Ica *Néni!*" I said.

Ica *Néni*, or Aunt Ica, told Tamás to hurry and get ready or we'd be late for school. Aunt Ica wasn't really my aunt, but in Hungary, we called all women "aunt" and all men "uncle."

Finally, Tamás was out the door. He and I often walked to school together, chatting happily, but we were unusually quiet that day. We desperately wanted to ask each other a question. The problem was, we knew that saying the wrong thing could be dangerous. We didn't even trust our friends completely.

In a Communist country such as ours, we had to be careful what we shared about our family's activities. Even a casual comment could get our parents into trouble, so we learned to guard our home lives. We had many secrets. Actually, almost everything was a secret. My father warned me never to talk about what he or my mother did or said at home, but today I was so worried, I knew I had to break this rule.

"Tamás," I said nervously, "is there something going on?"

"Like what?" he asked cautiously.

"Did your parents listen to Radio Free Europe last night?"

"My parents don't listen to Radio Free Europe. You know that's against the law!"

"Tamás, I'm so worried! I won't tell anyone what you said."

"Okay!" he said, his voice trembling. "They were up all night listening. And they've been whispering a lot for the past couple of days about something that's happening in Budapest. They stop talking when I come into the room."

"My parents, too. Whatever's happening is scary. I wish we didn't have to go to school."

"Let's stop talking and start walking, or we'll be late."

I could tell that Tamás was not comfortable with our conversation. We picked up our pace. All around us, people were milling in the streets, whispering and gesturing with their hands in an animated fashion.

"Perhaps there's no school today. No one seems to be going to work," I remarked.

"I overheard my father telling my mother about some parades. He said that the workers from most of the factories in town are marching to the ÁVH barracks today," Tamás said. "Maybe our teachers will allow us to leave school and join the march."

I wondered why anyone would want to go near the ÁVH barracks! The ÁVH was the organization of the Hungarian secret police. The police officers were called ÁVOs. Everyone was afraid of them! The ÁVOs spied on people and took them from their homes in the middle of the night. Sometimes they beat them up or arrested them for no reason at all.

We reached Tamás's school first, which was not too far from mine. Boys and girls did not attend the same school. I left Tamás and continued walking to my school. As I entered my classroom, I slipped my leather schoolbag off my back. The rest of my classmates were already there. The classroom was buzzing with conversation. Just like the people in the street, the kids in my class were also huddled together, whispering. Our teacher asked us to sit down and take out our notebooks. Each desk in the classroom seated two students. Beside me was one of my best friends, Zsuzsa. We started the day with our handwriting practice.

All good girls will join the Communist Party.

We wrote this sentence over and over. *I'm never joining the Party,* I thought. *My dad is not a member of the Party, and I won't be a member, either.* But I wasn't sure. Even thinking these thoughts was scary!

After our writing practice, we started our Russian lesson. I had just turned nine, and I was in the fourth grade. We started learning Russian that year. I didn't want to speak Russian. I wanted to learn English instead. My cousins in Canada spoke only English, and I wanted very much to write them letters and get to know them, especially Patsy, Connie, and Julie, who were my age.

As I was lost deep in thought, I heard a noise outside, on the street below. People were shouting and singing. Our teacher told us that we could go to the windows to have a look. We almost knocked one another over, trying to get a good view of what was going on outside.

Our classroom looked out on the main road of the town. The parade that Tamás had mentioned was going right past the school! From the window, I saw neighbors, friends, and workers from the Kühne factory, which made agricultural machines. My father worked there as an engineer and manager.

He was right at the front of the parade, carrying a Hungarian flag with a hole in its center. The Soviet symbol, which contained a red star, a hammer, and sheaves of wheat, had been cut out of the flag. Dad looked up and waved. I felt so proud! My Aunt Éva worked at the same factory. I caught sight of her near the end of the parade. She waved, as well. Hundreds of people were marching and singing the Hungarian anthem:

Isten, áldd meg a Magyart (God bless the Hungarian people)

Jó kedvvel, bőséggel, (With happiness and abundance,)

Nyújts feléje védő kart, (Offer your protective arm,)

Ha küzd ellenséggel. (If they should struggle with enemies.)

Oh, my God! I thought. *They shouldn't be singing the anthem.* Singing the Hungarian anthem could get people into a lot of trouble! After the Soviet Union took control of Hungary at the end of World War Two, the singing of the anthem was banned. The Soviets occupied our country and wanted Hungarians to forget who we were. We were expected to follow the rules and laws of the Soviet system and forget that we had our own culture and beliefs.

Anyone who disobeyed the Soviet rules was arrested. People were regularly arrested and charged with all kinds of "crimes" against the Communist government. The charges were seldom true, but it didn't matter. When people were arrested, their entire family suffered. Sometimes the family members couldn't get jobs or find places to live. The government owned all the factories and apartments and decided where people should work or live.

After the parade passed the school, our teacher called us back to our seats. Imagine my shock then, when she stood at attention and started singing the anthem! We also sang, our faces shining with love and stained with tears. In that moment, we felt we shared a secret we had guarded with our lives. We knew the words to the anthem! Our parents had taught us how to sing it, and in singing it, we *knew* we weren't Communists.

After we sang, a strange hush fell over the room. We had done something dangerous. Would anyone tell? Would anyone betray us? But I saw no traitors that day—only proud children like me. Our lessons ended around noon, and we packed up our books to go home.

This symbol appears above the center window of my old school. It is of two angels holding the Hungarian coat of arms (see page 25). I use this symbol later in the book.

From my classroom window, I could see the parade going by. My classroom was on the second floor, so I could see everyone clearly.

The man who kissed his friends that day

did not do it out of love.

His act was one of vicious cruelty!

His friends suffered the worst possible betrayal.

They paid for his friendship with their lives.

Though the sun shone brightly overhead,

a storm brewed inside people's hearts.

Tears spilled over their cheeks like rain,

Cleansing decades of grief from their souls.

Chapter Two

Tears Rained on the Town

I put my heavy schoolbag on my back and began walking home with my girlfriend Zsuzsa. Zsuzsa and I lived in the same apartment building. As we made our way down the steps, one of the teachers stopped us. She warned us not to take our usual route home. She suggested we take Csaba Street instead. Zsuzsa and I weren't rebellious, but we *were* curious!

"Let's go home along the main road, Zsuzsa," I said.

Zsuzsa nodded and replied, "I want to know what's happening, too."

So, we headed back along the route Tamás and I had taken early that morning. The hospital and police station were just ahead. As we got closer, we noticed that something was terribly wrong! People were walking slowly toward the hospital. Some were crying and covering their faces with their hands. Some leaned on others for support as they walked. Many had blood on their clothes. I saw a man propped up against a wall. He was smoking a cigarette. His shirt was ripped, and his arm was bare.

He had torn off his sleeve to make a bandage with the cloth. Blood covered the bandage, and more blood dripped down his arm. His eyes were unfocused. He was staring into space, somewhere very far away, as if he'd seen a ghost.

I thought I was seeing ghosts, too. All around us, people moved like zombies. Zsuzsa and I didn't dare speak or stop anyone to ask what was going on. We couldn't figure out what had happened. We stood among the injured, not knowing what to do next. We were terrified! A short distance away, I saw my mother riding her bicycle toward us. Zsuzsa and I ran to meet her.

"What happened, *Anyu* (Mom)?"

"The ÁVOs shot the people who marched on the ÁVH barracks this morning. That's all I know. Your father and your three aunts were planning to be part of that demonstration."

Suddenly, a thought ran through my head. *Was my father shot, too? Was he still alive?* I tried not to let my mother know what I was thinking, so I calmly told her that I *had* seen my father.

"I saw *Apu* (Dad) at the front of a parade. He was carrying a flag with a hole in it. I saw Éva, too, near the end of the parade."

My mother's face went white. I knew she had the same fear that I'd had about my father. Just then, an army ambulance drove up to the hospital, and the the gates opened. Right behind it were other ambulances, trucks, and wagons, all carrying wounded people. I heard people moaning, and I saw blood—so much blood! And there were tears. Tears spilled in rivers from people's eyes. Women were screaming the names of husbands, sons, and daughters who had been hurt, or perhaps even killed, and those who hadn't yet been found, like my father and aunts.

"Oh, my God!" my mother said. "I have to go into the hospital to see if your father and aunts are wounded. Babi, run and tell Grandmama what's happened. Tell her that I'm at the hospital and let her know why."

I did as my mother asked. Zsuzsa went home, and I ran to my grandmother's house as fast as I could. My grandparents lived in Károlyliget, on the outskirts of Mosonmagyaróvár. You had to cross a bridge to get there. Grandmama's house wasn't far from my school or our apartment building. I managed to reach it in less than ten minutes. I ran in the door, yelling at the top of my lungs.

"*Nagymama* (Grandmama)! Something bad has happened. There are hundreds of wounded people at the hospital. Dead people, too. And there's so much blood! I met Mom in front of the hospital, and she told me to tell you that she's going in there to look for Dad. Has anyone come home?" I asked.

My grandmother didn't answer me. She was praying. As I scanned the kitchen, I noticed my sister Zsuzsi huddled on a bench beside the stove, her face covered in tears. Grandmama motioned for me to sit beside her. Zsuzsi was two years younger than I was. She was sobbing and cradling my aunt Blanka's jacket. My aunts Éva, Blanka, and Marika were like big sisters to us. We didn't use the word "aunt" when we talked to them—we just called them by their names. Blanka and Éva were in their early twenties, and Marika was only nineteen.

Zsuzsi showed me a tear in the ruffles at the back of Blanka's jacket.

"Look at this bullet hole!" she cried.

I took the jacket from her. It was caked with blood and mud.

"Babi," Zsuzsi said sobbing, "Blanka almost died today."

Now it was my turn to hug the jacket. "Is she hurt? Tell me! Is she bleeding like all the others?"

Hearing the commotion, Blanka came into the room. Her face was ash gray, but thankfully, she didn't seem hurt. I jumped up and hugged her. I was very happy to see her alive! She was sobbing, so it was hard for her to speak. Finally, she composed herself and told me what had happened.

"More than a thousand people were marching to the ÁVH barracks this morning. The parades started out at several factories in town. Some people gathered in the city square in Magyaróvár.

People gathered at factories and at other places in town.

We wanted the ÁVOs to remove the Soviet stars from the barracks. Students and workers in Budapest have removed the red stars from buildings and cut the Soviet symbols out of Hungarian flags. We cut holes in our flags, too. The red star and other Communist symbols were added to our flag when the Soviet Union took over Hungary after World War Two."

"Did you cut a hole because the Soviet symbols don't really belong in our flag?"

"That's right, Babi," Blanka said. "And that means it isn't *really* a Hungarian flag.

"To continue my story, I was in the very first parade to arrive at the barracks. We were marching peacefully, singing the Hungarian anthem. In fact, a man at the front of the march waved a white flag to show that we were peaceful. He was greeted by an ÁVO, who came out of the barracks with his hands over his head to prove that he meant no harm, either. This ÁVO talked to some of the people he knew in the crowd. He smiled from ear to ear. He even kissed a couple of his friends.

"Then he returned to the barracks. He must have signaled to the people inside the building because, before anyone could figure out what was happening, more than twenty ÁVOs came outside and started firing at the crowd with machine guns. People were screaming, and many fell down. Bullets flew in all directions. One even went through the back of my jacket! Most of the people at the front of our parade were killed. The ÁVOs also threw hand grenades, killing many people behind me."

Blanka grew quiet. "I don't know how I survived!" she said. "I was right near the front. I remember diving into a muddy ditch and covering my head with my hands. A man fell on top of me. He must have been dead. I don't know who this man was, but he probably saved my life by shielding me from the gunfire. I can't even remember getting home."

"Did they shoot people for singing the anthem?" I asked.

Blanka told me the anthem was a part of a very complicated story. This was just as I had suspected! It meant that, in the eyes of the ÁVOs, I was guilty, too. I also sang the anthem this morning. *Would someone come and shoot me?*

All this talk of the anthem reminded me that my father had also been singing it as he marched past my school. I was growing frantic with worry about where he might be! My aunts Éva and Marika were missing, too, and my grandfather wasn't at home, either. Marika worked at the Bauxite plant with Blanka, but she was marching in the parade with another group of people, and Blanka said she hadn't see her.

"I'm going into town to find Éva and Marika," Blanka announced. "Promise me you won't leave the house!" she said to Zsuzsi and me sternly.

A couple of hours after Blanka left, Éva came home. We were happy to see her alive!

"Do you know that hundreds of people were killed and wounded at the ÁVH barracks today? Thank God, Imre (my father) and I didn't get there until *after* the shooting!"

The parade from the Bauxite factory, where Blanka and Marika worked, was the first to arrive. The Kühne factory was much farther from the barracks, so my father and Éva didn't get there until the shooting was over. Éva said that by the time they arrived, dead and wounded people were being loaded onto trucks. She spotted my dad in the crowd. She was frantic with worry.

People told Dad and Éva that the wounded and dead were being taken to the hospital. They decided to go there to look for my aunts. The first thing they saw when they arrived was my mother going from body to body, looking for my father and her sisters. She was so relieved when she saw my father and Éva, that she almost fainted. Éva asked her if she'd seen Marika or Blanka, but Mom shook her head. Mom and Dad stayed at the hospital to look for them and sent Éva home to tell us the news.

This memorial is one of several that can be found in Magyaróvár today. It is in front of the old fort and pays respect to the college students who died in the 1956 massacre.

Inside the hospital, there was total chaos! Doctors and other healthcare workers were struggling tirelessly to save lives. One of those doctors was a man named Dr. Székelyhidi László, who married my Aunt Joli several years later.

Although he wanted to be a doctor working in a hospital, the government gave my Uncle "Laci" a job as a physician at the army barracks in Magyaróvár. The army barracks were a little more than a half mile (1 km) from the ÁVH headquarters. At eleven o'clock on Friday morning, Uncle Laci heard shots being fired, followed by a couple of explosions. On hearing the shots, he knew exactly where they were being fired. He'd heard about the parades that were going to the ÁVH barracks that day.

He and some other medical staff and soldiers immediately drove army ambulances and other vehicles to the barracks. When Uncle Laci arrived at the ÁVH headquarters, he couldn't believe what he saw! In front of the barracks, the fields and ditches were strewn with bodies. Wounded people were screaming with pain. Many others were motionless. Those who were not wounded were either in shock or running for their lives. They were fleeing because no one was sure if the shooting had finished.

Uncle Laci told the soldiers that they first needed to find the wounded. Because some were unconscious, the men had to check the pulses of anyone who wasn't moving. Other soldiers bandaged the wounds of those who were bleeding and helped them into the ambulances and army trucks. Many of the wounds were severe. The soldiers did their best to stop the bleeding.

A few people who took part in the demonstration and were not hurt stayed to help load the injured onto trucks, wagons, carts, and any other vehicles they could find.

The wounded were taken into the hospital building. There were so many, that there weren't enough beds for them all. Men, women, and children lay on the hallway floor. There was blood everywhere! The hospital staff had never handled this type of emergency before and needed help. All healthcare workers and any civilians who were willing to assist came to the hospital to give the doctors a hand.

Before treating the wounded, the healthcare workers had to ask the patients questions about their medical conditions and find out their bloodtypes. The most badly wounded were prepped for surgery right away. Many people lost arms or legs that day. The less serious wounds were cleaned and bandaged.

The hospital administrators in Magyaróvár called the hospital in Győr for emergency assistance. The city of Győr is about a half hour from Magyaróvár by car. It had a bigger hospital, more doctors, and was better-equipped for surgery. The ambulances from Győr brought bandages and badly needed medicines. They also brought doctors. The ambulances then returned to Győr with some of the seriously wounded patients.

The medical staff worked feverishly throughout that day and night, treating between 150 and 200 injured people. They were exhausted and feeling very sad. It wasn't until dawn that they had a chance to take a deep breath and talk about the day's events.

When their patients were stabilized, the healthcare workers sat down and quietly asked one another the question, "What just happened here?" And then, as if their hearts suddenly broke at once, they all screamed out one word. "Why?"

The scream echoed throughout the town. Everyone was asking why, and no one had any answers.

Those who died were laid out in the courtyard of the hospital in a covered enclosure. Many were so coated with mud and blood that their loved ones couldn't recognize them. The grandmothers of Magyaróvár, including mine, heard this and came to help the next day. With gentle hands and loving hearts, they washed the faces and bodies of these innocent sons and daughters of our town. They grieved them as they would grieve their own family members.

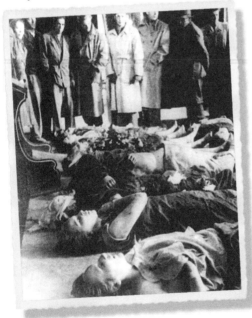

(left) The people who died during the massacre were laid out in the courtyard of the hospital. Family members came to look for their missing loved ones.

Map of Mosonmagyaróvár in 1956

TO AUSTRIA

TO CZECHOSLOVAKIA

TO GYŐR

N

Small Lajta

9

6

7

8

10

2

3

1

4

5

1 School

2 Hospital

POLICE 3 Police Station

4 Grandparents' house

5 ÁVH Barracks

6 City Hall

7 My home

8 Church

9 Fort

10 Cemetery

When bad things happen,

people need the basic comforts of home and food.

My grandmother's food was cooked with love.

It nourished our bodies and fed our souls.

It allowed us to be together

to talk around the table.

We knew that if we were hungry,

we were still alive.

Chapter Three

Food for Body and Soul

While our parents were at the hospital, Zsuzsi and I were waiting with Grandmama and Éva. It was hard to sit and wait for our missing family members. We desperately wanted them home. When Grandmama realized how worried Zsuzsi and I were, she put us to work.

"Let's cook dinner for the family!" she suggested. "They'll be starving when they get home."

Zsuzsi and I jumped at the chance to do something other than worry. Éva was eager to help, too. Cooking would take her mind off the events of the day. My grandmother had bought some beef the day before and was planning to make *gulyás*, or goulash, for dinner. My sister and I climbed a ladder to the pantry, which was in the attic above the kitchen, and brought down some potatoes and onions. Zsuzsi peeled the potatoes, and I peeled the onions. Peeling onions made me cry, and Zsuzsi was close enough to the onion fumes that she started crying, as well. But we were happy to be crying "onion tears" for a change. It made us laugh.

Éva cut the meat into little pieces and then chopped the onions and potatoes we had peeled. Grandmama took out a big pot and put in a generous helping of lard, which is animal fat. When the lard melted, Éva threw in the chopped onions and some garlic she had smashed with a knife. Immediately, the kitchen was filled with the most wonderful aroma! Grandmama stirred the onions and added the meat. She dusted the meat and onions with salt, flour, and paprika. Hungarians love paprika! After the meat had browned, it was time to add water to the goulash. We didn't have running water at Grandmama's house, so Éva had to pump it from the well, which was just outside the kitchen door.

Éva then filled a large pitcher with water and poured the water into the goulash pot. The goulash needed to simmer for at least a half hour before Grandmama put in the potatoes. She also prepared dumplings from flour, lard, an egg, and water, which she added to the goulash later. As far as I was concerned, the dumplings were the very best part!

While the goulash simmered, we helped Grandmama bake a plum cake. *How is it*, I wondered, *that we always feel loved in this kitchen?* Grandmama seemed to put her love into the food she cooked, and we showed our love by eating the food with great joy!

I suppose it made perfect sense that we cooked and baked that day and talked about our family. Grandmama told us that she had a feeling everyone was safe.

"Mothers know," she said, "if something is wrong with their children. And I feel no such thing!"

And the best part? She was right! It wasn't long before my parents, aunts, and grandfather walked through the door. Everyone was alive! Grandpapa sniffed the air like a dog. Then he winked at Zsuzsi and me. "Thank God, Babi and Zsuzsi decided to cook dinner. We're starving!"

Everyone laughed, of course, for the first time that day. But we ate quietly at our large kitchen table, savoring the delicious food and feeling thankful that we were together. What a blessing that no one in our family was killed. No one was even hurt!

"Marika and Grandpapa, where were you?" I asked. "We were so worried about you!"

Marika told us that she had gone to work that morning, as usual. She knew about the parade because people all over Hungary were marching to support what was happening in Budapest. She even joined her company's group in the march, but almost instantly, she had a strong sense of dread. Desperately, she tried to find Blanka. She wanted to talk her sister out of going, as well. But it was a huge crowd, and Blanka was nowhere to be found. Marika smiled across the table at her sister.

"So what could I do? I went home to wait for Miklós."

Blanka had been worried that Marika might be wounded, or even dead. After she left Grandmama's, she searched for Marika everywhere. She met my parents at the hospital, but they hadn't found her, either. Then, on a hunch, Blanka thought she should check Marika's room!

Since they got married, Marika and her husband Miklós had been living in a house very close to where my grandparents lived. Blanka found Marika asleep in her room. She woke her and told her the terrible news about the massacre. The sisters hugged each other and cried.

We then found out that my grandfather had been at home all along! He'd spent the afternoon glued to the radio in the back room of the house. We had no idea that he'd been there. As was his habit, he'd closed the curtains and lowered the volume on the radio. This may seem strange, but it wasn't all that surprising. Whenever my grandfather listened to Radio Free Europe, he always covered his tracks (see page 22).

Many people, including my grandfather, received news about the rest of the world through Radio Free Europe. But listening to this station was against the law in Hungary because the news couldn't be censored, or controlled by the Communists. The government didn't want Hungarians to know what was happening in other parts of the world, especially in the West. The West included the non-Communist countries of Europe and North and South America. When people started thinking about the West, they also thought about freedom—and freedom was not what the Soviet Union had in mind for Hungarians. Grandpapa didn't want us to know that he was listening to Radio Free Europe, so we wouldn't have to lie if someone asked us.

This was my grandparents' house, where I was born. My grandfather listened to the radio in the room on the left. The kitchen was at the other end of the house, so we couldn't hear him.

"Enough is enough!" the people cried.
This land is ours.
We have rights, and we have a history.
We have our own culture and traditions.
We need to be ourselves again.
Our hearts and minds know
what we want and need.
We are not Russians.
We are the Magyar people.

Chapter Four

The Revolution in Budapest

I had so many questions and fears! "Why were those people shot? How could that secret police officer smile and kiss his friends and then shoot them? Was the same thing happening in Budapest, our capital city? Were people there also hurt?"

My father sighed when he heard all my questions. It had been a long day, and he was exhausted. He must have realized that even the short version of what happened in our capital city would involve some explanation.

"The Revolution started in Budapest on Tuesday night," he started telling the story.

"What's a revolution?" my sister and I asked in unison.

"It's going to be a long night if you two keep interrupting," he replied. But he smiled warmly, and then he went on.

"A revolution is like a war against a ruler or a political system. Our country is ruled by the Soviet Union, and the political system is Communism. The Soviet Union has a Communist government, but Hungarians don't want to be Communists."

We nodded in agreement. Zsuzsi and I didn't want to be Communists, either. Zsuzsi was too young, but I belonged to the Communist youth group called Young Pioneers. I had no choice. I had to wear my red neckerchief to school every day. Red is the color of Communism.

The Young Pioneer leaders taught us the principles of Communism and warned us never to stray from these principles—or we'd surely be punished. I understood that I had to pretend to believe in Communism in order to stay safe.

My father went on with his story.

"The Revolution really started in Szeged, my home town. Students there staged a demonstration to protest the Communist system. They formed their own political organization and sent representatives to Budapest. They wanted students from all over Hungary to join their new organization, which they called Mefész.

"Students at the Budapest Technical University joined Mefész, too, and drew up a list of 16 demands they wanted to read to the government. On the night of Tuesday, October 23rd, thousands of students and other people in Budapest gathered together to read this list of demands. The demands are changes that the students want the Hungarian government to make. They want more freedom and free elections. Under Communism, there are no elections. People are told who their leaders will be. The students also demanded that a new government be formed.

"The students want other changes, too," my father said. "Important changes. They want the right to think and speak freely. And, most important of all, they want the ÁVH to be dismantled and the Soviets to leave Hungary.

"The students marched to the National Radio Building to read their demands over the air. But when the protesters arrived at the radio station, the ÁVH fired bullets into the crowd! Several people were killed, and many more were injured. This injustice infuriated the protesters! Together, they toppled a huge statue of Stalin and dragged it through the streets."

My father paused. "Babi," he said, "do you know who this man, Stalin, was?"

"Yes," I said. "He was a Soviet leader."

"He was a horrible dictator," my father replied. "He ordered the murders of thousands of innocent people."

"I'm glad they knocked his statue down," I said in return.

He nodded. "Unfortunately, this wasn't a victory for the protesters. Not only were many people wounded and killed, but on the following day, October 24th, Soviet tanks rolled into Budapest. The government said the tanks were sent in to 'restore order.' Then, a surprising thing happened. The Hungarian army started helping the freedom fighters.

"The next night, protesters gathered in front of the Parliament Buildings, demanding that Imre Nagy appear. Imre Nagy had been the prime minister of Hungary a few years before and was a much better leader than the other Hungarian leaders had been.

"But as the crowd waited, several ÁVOs lined up on the roof of the Parliament Buildings. It wasn't long before they started firing, and hundreds more people were killed."

"That sounds just like what happened here," we piped in, "in Magyaróvár!"

"That's right. Only we didn't expect anything like that to happen in our small city!"

I knew that things must have been very bad in Budapest. People there were in real danger—people like my Aunt Joli, who was also my godmother. Aunt Joli, Uncle János, and their two baby girls, Nori and Lilla, lived in Budapest. We'd received no news from them and prayed they were still alive!

The ÁVOs lined up on the roof of the Parliament Buildings in Budapest and fired on the crowd. Hundreds of people were wounded and killed.

(above) Huge crowds gathered in Budapest to support the students' demands. They carried the revolutionary flag with a hole in its center.

(below) The angry protesters pulled down Stalin's statue.

There are really only two emotions.

They are love and fear.

When you send fear outward,

it is anger.

When you hold it in,

it is sadness.

The greatest fear in Hungary that week

was the fear of losing control.

People showed that fear in both ways.

Chapter Five

The Day After in Magyaróvár

That night Zsuzsi and I slept at my grandparents' house.

"You're safer here," my father said. "Lenin Street may be dangerous now."

Our apartment was on Lenin Street. It was the main road leading in and out of Magyaróvár between Budapest and Vienna, Austria. Our home was almost directly across from City Hall. I didn't want to sleep away from my parents, especially after a day of worrying about my father, but I knew better than to argue.

"We're coming home first thing in the morning!" I insisted. "We can walk home with Grandmama when she goes to church."

My parents agreed. I hardly slept that night, and I couldn't wait to hear the rooster crow. He started making a racket at around five each morning, which was when my grandfather woke up. Grandpapa had a daily ritual of making coffee for the family and shining everyone's shoes. He always lined them up in the kitchen before any of us were awake.

"You have to put your best foot forward!" he'd say, smiling.

The next morning, I was up with him and the rooster. I fetched some water for the coffee and helped him shine the shoes. What a relief it was to be busy and not to have to worry about what might happen that day!

Grandpapa gave me some bread and cherry jam for breakfast. We had many cherry trees, and Grandmama made delicious jam from the fruit. I also ate a handful of fresh walnuts that I had helped my grandmother shell the week before.

By six o'clock, the whole house was awake. Everyone was happy that the coffee was ready. Grandmama made the adults eggs for breakfast. Marika and Miklós came for breakfast, as well. It was Saturday, which was a workday in Hungary, but no one knew whether or not they should be going to work. While talking over breakfast, we decided to walk over to our apartment to see what was happening in town. More than anything, Zsuzsi and I wanted to be with our parents.

Grandmama went to church at eight o'clock, and the rest of us continued walking to our apartment. Hundreds of people were on our street by then, shouting, their fists pounding the air. They were dangerously angry! We ran upstairs to our apartment. My mother and father were leaning out the corner window, watching the crowd gathering below. People always gathered across the road at City Hall to find out the latest news.

My father told us that, after the shooting the day before, some people returned to the ÁVH barracks and killed two of the ÁVOs. A third ÁVO was beaten very badly. He was in the hospital with severe injuries. But it turned out that István Dudás, the man who had given the orders to fire on the crowd, and his top men, were long gone by the time the crowd arrived. They were in hiding.

"I think there's going to be more trouble," my dad said. "Look at the people in front of City Hall! I don't know what's going on, but when I was down there earlier, some men were talking about storming the hospital and hanging the injured ÁVO who is now a patient there."

As he said this, we saw a large group of people heading toward the hospital. They were going there to confront the injured ÁVO for his part in the killings. When they arrived, they found the wounded officer in bed, his head covered in bandages. A soldier was guarding him. Some of the people who were part of the crowd had lost relatives in the massacre and felt the ÁVO shouldn't be allowed to live. The doctors tried to calm the crowd by saying that the man had suffered severe injuries and probably wouldn't live long anyway. Someone in the crowd then asked the ÁVO, point blank, if he would ever hurt anyone again.

"I would kill a thousand more of you!" he spat out at them.

On hearing this reply, the crowd dragged the man out and hanged him by his feet in front of a nearby church. The doctors were right. The man didn't live very long.

Back at City Hall, the crowd grew even bigger! We stayed by our corner window to watch what was happening. Meanwhile, my father and Uncle Miklós went down to the street to talk to some people they knew.

As we watched from our window, a group of people entered the gates of City Hall. It wasn't long before they were dragging a man through the gates. The man was an ÁVO who was being held prisoner at City Hall. He had tried to escape by jumping from a second-floor window that faced the courtyard of the building. As he was getting up from his fall, the crowd grabbed him and dragged him out to the street. They killed him right there, using their feet. When my mother finally spoke, her voice was flat.

"Another man is dead," was all she said.

I knew how she felt. I had seen the anger and felt the hatred of the people below, and it made me sick. Another man was dead. And though this man had killed other men, women, and children, no one in my family was happy about his death. We knew that violence would lead only to more violence.

Why was there so much hatred? And who else would have to die before the end of the day—or the end of the week? Would it be someone I knew and loved? I was sure that the man who had just been killed had family and friends who loved him. Perhaps his death was the result of his beliefs. He believed in an idea that was based on fear and lies. What if he was as scared as the rest of us— scared not to follow the orders that he'd been given?

In Hungary, most people were afraid to say what they really felt. I know I was. At school, we feared we might say something wrong. Even worse, we feared that our teacher might take this "wrong" thing to the secret police.

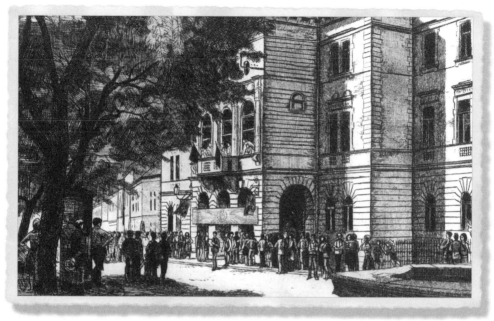

When people gathered at City Hall, we could see what was happening from our corner window.

our lookout window

City Hall

NAPOLEON

Being afraid to think or speak freely was a heavy burden to carry. No wonder people were angry! More than anything, they wanted to scream out the thoughts they were too afraid to say. They didn't want to be afraid anymore, and they wanted the Soviets to know it.

That night, I wanted to sleep at our apartment with my parents. I begged my mother to let me stay. Sleeping, however, was next to impossible. Directly across the street from our building was the funeral home. Throughout the night, we heard banging sounds, as if a construction crew was working there. Tap, tap! Bang, bang! The noise went on and on. The noise, we finally realized, was the hammering together of coffins. A mass funeral was scheduled for the following day.

Almost a hundred people were buried at the funeral. I imagined how sad it must have been for the mourners to lose their family members and friends. Death is especially hard to accept when you don't expect it! No one expected their loved ones to die that Friday. The most heartbroken were the parents who had lost children. Several children were killed during the massacre.

I went to the cemetery a few days after the funeral and saw the freshly dug graves. In the cemetery, as well as in town, I saw people wearing black clothes or black armbands. Black is the color of mourning. Everyone seemed to be mourning loved ones! After that day, I saw black armbands everywhere I looked. The armbands are a reminder that we must never forget that Friday. Each one of us still carries the huge loss within our hearts.

A mass funeral was held on the Sunday after the massacre. We will never forget the people who died. When I see a black armband, I always think of them.

Wooden markers and a memorial are reminders of the massacre that took place in front of this building, which was once the ÁVH barracks. The posts symbolize those who were killed.

Communist rule turned our country gray.

There was a lack of color in our lives.

Freedom surrounded us with rainbows.

The colors of our new world

made us feel real.

They made us feel happy and free.

The colors allowed us to see

what could be.

Chapter Six

Six Days of Freedom

That Sunday, while the people of Magyaróvár were burying their dead, news came from Budapest that the Soviet tanks were leaving the country. Such good news on such a sad day! Hungary had finally won its freedom. The freedom fighters fought bravely against both the ÁVOs and the Soviet troops and had destroyed many of their tanks with Molotov cocktails. Children as young as twelve were throwing these homemade bombs and were fighting bravely in the streets.

Beautiful Budapest was a mess! Streets were torn up, and windows and walls were riddled with bullet holes. Despite all this, most people felt that their freedom was worth the fight. Many ÁVOs had been killed, and others had left the country or were in hiding. To stay safe, some even pretended to be freedom fighters.

During the happy days of celebration that followed, the Austrian-Hungarian borders opened for the first time in many years. Under Communist rule, people had not been free to come and go as they pleased. Watchtowers and barbed-wire fences had been put up, closing off the borders to outsiders. This guarded border was called the "Iron Curtain."

Once the borders were open, people from Western Europe and North America came to Hungary to see firsthand if the Soviets had actually left. They took photographs and cheered on the victorious freedom fighters. Since Magyaróvár was very close to the Austrian border, the visitors stopped in our town on their way to Budapest. Foreigners speaking German, English, or French filled the streets of the town. The visitors gathered at the Fekete Sas Tavern. *Fekete Sas* means Black Eagle. The tavern was right beside City Hall and visible from our window.

Many of the foreigners were journalists. They came to write stories for their newspapers and magazines. Before leaving our town, they attended the mass funeral. The massacre that took place in Magyaróvár horrified them! Almost all the journalists wrote stories about the massacre because of the cold-blooded way in which the ÁVOs had killed innocent, unarmed people.

My father enjoyed talking to the Westerners. He spoke only a few words of German, but he was very charming. He always found ways to communicate. First thing every morning, he was out in the street mingling with the journalists. It was there that he met two women from France. One was a university professor, and the other was her student.

In the past, Magyaróvár had little need for hotels because no one ever visited from outside the country. This meant that the visitors had nowhere to stay. The people of Magyaróvár rose to this challenge. Soon, every foreign guest was put up at someone's home. My family welcomed into our home the two French women my father met. Their names were Celia and Danielle.

In those days, most people in Hungary lived in tiny apartments. Those who belonged to the Communist Party were given the best apartments. Although we weren't members of the Party, my family had an unusually large apartment. It was made up of three big rooms, with a bathroom across the hall. The three main rooms were connected to one another by double doors. When these doors were opened, the place could hold more than a hundred people for a party. My parents had many friends, and they often hosted parties on New Year's Eve.

After my mother made a delicious dinner for our guests, we sat down and talked with them. We learned that Celia could speak German, English, and French, as well as Hungarian. She was born in Hungary but had lived in France most of her life. Danielle's parents owned several large department stores in Paris.

Danielle was studying Political Science at university and begged Celia to bring her to Hungary so that she could experience a real revolution. Celia saw no harm in coming to Hungary now that the Revolution was over. The two women planned to go to Budapest—the scene of the action, but the trains weren't running. So, they stayed at our apartment for a few days.

Celia asked me if I liked school. I told her I loved it! I always had the highest or second-highest marks in my class. This past year, I'd won the top prize. It was a book on Lenin.

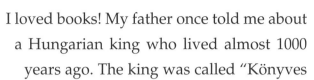

I loved books! My father once told me about a Hungarian king who lived almost 1000 years ago. The king was called "Könyves Kálmán," or "Kalman the Booklover." Dad said that I was "Kálmán Babi the Booklover" because I read so much.

When I told Celia about my prize, she said, "You don't need your Lenin book anymore! Forget the Communist propaganda they taught you!"

My father nodded and said, "Burn your Lenin book!"

I almost fainted. How could he suggest something so awful?

"Are you kidding?" I said, smiling. I was sure he was. But he said, "No! Just put it into the stove. We'll use it as a fire starter."

I felt a bit ashamed that I wanted to keep my book, so I put it into an unlit stove while they watched. The weather was so warm, we didn't have to heat the apartment yet, so I wasn't worried that my parents would burn the book that night. The next day, when no one was at home, I rescued it and hid it under my bed.

I wanted to keep my prize, and I hated the idea of burning *any* book, but I also thought I loved Lenin! I learned to think one way at home and another way at school. At school, I was taught that Lenin was a hero.

Lenin had been the first premier of the Soviet Union and a revolutionary leader. He wanted to give power to the common people and take it away from the rich. Of course, I would later learn that Lenin was not worthy of my admiration! He started the secret police and put many innocent people into labor camps, where most of them died.

Aside from discussions about Lenin, I talked with Celia about a lot of things. She inspired me to think big thoughts about what my life could be. She challenged me and made me believe in myself. Sometimes it takes just one person to give you the courage to know that your dreams can come true, and with Celia's help, I knew that I had that power.

I couldn't wait to wake up each morning! Each day brought so many surprises! People kept pouring into our country from the West, introducing us to things we'd never seen before. As I came out of my apartment building one morning, for example, I noticed a white van with a red cross was parked on the street. A crowd of people surrounded the van. I ran over to see what was going on, and a woman inside handed me an orange. I'd never seen one before! I thanked her and ran to school with my treasure.

As usual, I was the last to arrive, but it didn't seem to matter. None of the students were sitting at their desks. They, too, were marveling at some fruit they had just received! We discussed what to do with these novelties. My girlfriend Margit bit into the skin of her banana, which was like rubber. She said it didn't taste very good. Someone suggested she peel the banana, but she couldn't figure out how to do it. Finally, the teacher showed her.

In front of us, Margit pulled the peel down, one strip after another, until we could see the soft fruit underneath. The smell reminded me of pudding. Margit said the banana was sweeter than anything she'd ever tasted. In that moment, I so wished I'd received a banana, but then I wouldn't have had my orange!

I inhaled the aroma of my orange. It smelled so wonderful that I found myself wishing I had a perfume made of the scent. Like Margit, I also didn't know how to eat my fruit. I wondered if an orange was like a lemon that you had to cut in half and squeeze. I *had* seen lemons in Hungary from time to time. Finally, I bit into the skin and made a face. The bitterness of the skin surprised me! I finally figured out how to peel the orange, and I ate the sections slowly, one by one. How delicious they tasted!

Everyone in class was so giddy with happiness, that the teacher didn't want to ruin our fun by making us study. We didn't open a book and were not even given homework. We just sat around and talked all morning. We told one another about the foreign guests staying in our homes. Almost all of us had one or two, but I was the only one who had a university professor.

I told my friends that, like Celia, I was going to learn several languages. I thought I might even become a teacher. I asked *our* teacher which language she thought we'd be learning, now that the Soviets had left. Zsuzsa said she hoped it would be German because she was already fluent in it. I hoped it would be English, so I could write to my cousins in Canada.

That was the best day I'd ever spent in school! On the way home, I bumped into Tamás. I told him about the fun we'd had with our teacher. His experience had been very different. His teacher had warned his students not to get too used to having freedom. He said the Soviet tanks would come back before long.

Tamás added nervously, "I hope the Soviets don't come back!"

Although this thought had crept into our minds, most of us were too happy to consider the possibility.

"But Tamás, Imre Nagy won't let them come back," I said.

"The Soviets don't ask permission," he reminded me.

I didn't like where this conversation was heading, so I tried to distract him with a cool observation.

"Why is Imre Nagy such a good prime minister?"

"Is this one of your dumb riddles?"

"It's not a riddle," I said. "It's like a good omen. Imre is *my* father's first name, and Nagy is *your* father's last name. Imre Nagy is a combination of our two fathers. Both our fathers are good men, so Imre Nagy must be a wonderful man!"

Of course, Tamás loved the thought that this man who had our fathers' names was running the country. We agreed that Imre Nagy would do an excellent job!

"Let's enjoy our freedom and our new lives," I said. "Think about all the things you want to do and have, and your dreams will come true. Nothing can stop us if we believe in our dreams!"

Tamás rolled his eyes and said, "Dream a new bike for me, will you?"

I never knew about human rights
or that I lived without most of them.
I never knew that it was my right to live without
fear or discrimination or force.
I never knew about having the right to own
property or to get an education of my choice or
about the right to leave my country.
I never knew about the right to speak my mind
or the right to be proud of my culture.
I didn't know I had the right to choose
what I thought was right for me.
I never knew I had the right to be free.

Chapter Seven

The End of Our Freedom

Not everyone was as confident as I was that our freedom would last. Some people were waiting for "the other shoe to drop." My grandfather spent hours listening to the radio, and he didn't like what he was hearing. The radio stations in various parts of Hungary were reporting that they had seen Soviet tanks in the countryside. These tanks were supposed to have left! In some border towns, people also noticed that tanks were *coming into* Hungary rather than *leaving*. Still, we remained optimistic.

Since Sunday, October 28th, Hungarians had been crossing the border back and forth between Austria and Hungary. One day, my father went to Vienna, Austria's capital city, on his motorcycle. He came back raving about what a beautiful city Vienna was. He promised to take us over for a visit soon. There was a problem with money, however. Hungary's currency, the Forint, was almost worthless in Austria, or in any country that wasn't under Soviet rule. Without money, we couldn't buy anything or do very much outside Hungary.

It was now Saturday, November 3rd, and all seemed right with the world. There were many wonderful things to think about, and much to look forward to. On Sunday, we planned to go to church with my grandparents and then have a huge lunch at their house. Grandmama was making my favorite meal—fried chicken. I knew that she'd have something wonderful for dessert, too. I couldn't wait to eat one of my grandmother's Sunday feasts!

That night, there was a lot of noise that sounded like thunder. Naturally, I assumed it was a part of my dream, but what I woke up to the next morning was my worst nightmare! Parked in front of our building was a huge Soviet tank. And what we'd heard during the night was the roll of *hundreds* just like it! The tanks came into Hungary across the Czechoslovakian border, which was about the same distance from Magyaróvár as the Austrian border was.

Tamás had been right. The Soviets did come back! My heart froze. In fact, everything inside me went cold. Would I have to forget all my dreams? Would my world lose all its colors and once again become gray? Freedom was addictive, and I wondered if Hungarians could live without it. Surely not now—not anymore! When it came to freedom, I knew I was hooked.

My parents stood by the window, looking at the tank. Hardly anyone was out on the street. The familiar smell of fear was back. It filled my nostrils and constricted my throat! My parents wondered aloud if we should leave our home and go to church, as planned. My mother finally decided.

The Soviet tank sat right in front of our apartment building. Our apartment was on the top floor. Zsuzsi and I had a good look at the tank on our way to church. You can see the church's red roof behind our building.

"Yes," she said, "we'll go to church. Prayers always help!"

Grandmama and my aunts arrived at the same time we did, so we went in together. They told us that, on their way to church, they had passed a tank on Magyar Street. We told them that we had a tank sitting *right in front of our home* and that Zsuzsi and I had a good look at it.

Grandmama whispered to us that Grandpapa was listening to Radio Free Europe. I knew this was a secret and, in that moment, all I could think about were the secrets and lies of the past. Would I again have to keep secrets and tell lies?

Everyone has secrets. Secrets are about our inner worlds. They can be ideas or dreams that we want to keep to ourselves. But the kind of secrets I hated were the ones that I *had* to keep so that I, or others I loved, wouldn't get hurt. These secrets made me lie when I wanted to tell the truth. They made me feel bad because I realized that someone or something else controlled my life and my truth. I swore to myself that I wouldn't keep these secrets anymore. Not anymore!

During our week of freedom, we had dared to hope. How could we go back to our old way of life? It didn't seem possible now. I knew that a change had taken place inside me. My brush with freedom gave me power. I decided right then and there that I would still do all the things I dreamt of doing. My dreams were messages from the deepest part of my being. I wasn't sure how, but I knew I had to hold on to those dreams!

Mass was over, but I hardly heard a word of it because I was so deep in thought. We left the church and went to Grandmama's house. Grandmama and Éva had prepared a wonderful lunch. There was a mountain of fried chicken, a huge bowl of mashed potatoes, and lots of cucumber salad. For dessert, Éva had baked a *dobos torta*, a cake with many layers and a hard caramel topping.

My father went to the back room to listen to the radio with my grandfather. When they came into the kitchen a while later, I could tell that the news was not good. They told us that, early in the morning, Soviet troops had attacked Budapest. The fighting in the streets had resumed. The radio station was sending SOS, or distress signals, to the United Nations and the United States. Hungary was desperate for help! Would the United States help us?

Meanwhile, at the army barracks in Magyaróvár, some Soviet soldiers in tanks stopped and asked my Uncle Laci for directions to the Suez Canal. Evidently, the soldiers had been told that they were going to Egypt to help fight a war and had no idea they were in Hungary! My uncle pulled out a map to show them where they *really* were. The Soviet government had lied to the soldiers because they knew that the soldiers wouldn't want to help crush a revolution. Their countries were under Soviet occupation, just as our country was. Our struggle was their struggle, too.

Wind challenged Sun to a contest.

He bragged that he could remove a man's coat

by the force of his blows.

Sun accepted the challenge with a smile.

Wind blew and blew and blew.

The stronger his blows,

the tighter the man's grip on his coat.

Wind blew even harder.

The man held on even tighter.

Then it was Sun's turn.

She beamed her warm smile on the man.

Feeling her warmth, the man took off his coat.

In the end, can force ever win over true power?

Chapter Eight

The Reign of Terror

Hungary now had a new leader, János Kádár. Kádár was a traitor to the Hungarian people. Up until then, he was part of Imre Nagy's government and called himself Nagy's best friend.

When the Soviet tanks came into Budapest on November 4th, Imre Nagy sought asylum, or protection, at the Yugoslav Embassy. János Kádár then betrayed Nagy in the worst possible way! He convinced Nagy that he would be safe if he left the embassy. But, as soon as Nagy stepped out of the embassy, Kádár had him arrested and taken to Romania. Nagy was brought back to Hungary a couple of years later and executed under the orders of his so-called friend.

After taking over, János Kádár wasted no time in unleashing a reign of terror! He empowered the ÁVOs to punish first and ask questions later. The ÁVOs now had the right to arrest and hurt or kill anyone they suspected of anything! The ÁVOs hanged hundreds of freedom fighters. They took thousands more from their homes and beat them almost to death.

Photographs, which had been taken in Hungary by the journalists from the West, were used as proof of treason. Many people were accused of being traitors, or acting against the government, simply because they appeared in some photographs. The West was the government's enemy, and those who associated with Westerners were now considered enemies, too.

The ÁVOs didn't bother to listen to the people they arrested. They fabricated, or made up, reasons for the arrests and pronounced people guilty according to their own whims. Even worse, they took people from their homes in the middle of the night—a true sign of cowardice! Someone who is half asleep is unlikely to think straight, let alone fight back.

Many horror stories circulated throughout our town. One particularly sad story was about the father of one of my friends. The ÁVOs arrested him one night and beat him very badly. His entire back was covered in bloody welts. The ÁVOs claimed they arrested him because he went to Budapest to fight in the Revolution. In reality, he went on vacation *near* Budapest a week before the Revolution. When he learned about the Revolution, he tried to come home but couldn't. There was no train or bus service out of Budapest at that time.

After his arrest and beating, my friend's father was no longer allowed to work in Magyaróvár. He had to leave town and move to Budapest to find a job. His family couldn't go with him because his wife's parents, who lived in Magyaróvár, needed her support. My friend's father died in Budapest just five years later.

We worried a lot about my father's safety, as well. My father was a manager at the Kühne factory and was a very important person, both at the company and in town. Even the Communists recognized his importance. After the Revolution, they relied on him to get people at the factory back to work.

During the month of November, there were strikes and other protests that meant the Revolution was still not completely over. Business in Hungary was not nearly back to normal. Because people respected my father, the Communists realized it was better to have him working than to beat him senseless. If you were useful to the Communists, you were safe—at least for a little while. But how long before they turned on my father, too? He had always refused to join the Communist Party, and now he had other things to hide. The ÁVOs could never find out, for example, that he was helping foreigners and freedom fighters leave Hungary!

Tens of thousands of people were now leaving Hungary. Most of these people became refugees in Austria. As soon as the trains were up and running to and from Budapest again, refugees with heavy suitcases crowded onto them daily. In addition to clothes, their suitcases held prized possessions—anything, such as artwork or photographs, that people couldn't bear to leave behind, or which they could sell outside Hungary to earn some money.

Since there was such a lack of order in Hungary at this time, it took a while for the Soviets and ÁVOs to deal with the refugee situation. At first, they didn't try to stop people from leaving. Many Hungarians crossed the Austrian border near a town named

Sopron. It was relatively easy to walk across the border there—that is, until the Hungarian government closed it down. People also came to our town. From Magyaróvár, the refugees took a bus to Hegyeshalom, a village that was right at the border.

That's how my aunt Blanka left. She didn't tell anyone that she was planning to leave because she didn't want to give my grandparents or her sisters a chance to change her mind. One day, she simply came into the kitchen with her packed bags in hand and announced that she was leaving Hungary.

"I've had enough," she said. "I didn't almost lose my life to be back where I started. Things are even worse now than they were before. I can't stay. I can't!"

We were in a state of shock! Nobody had a clue that Blanka was leaving—and we had so little time to say goodbye. Later that night, Blanka took a bus to Hegyeshalom and, with hundreds of other Hungarians, walked across the border. Her plan was to go to her cousin Rózsi's apartment in Vienna and apply for immigration papers for Canada from there.

Rózsi was the daughter of my grandfather's sister, who had married an Austrian. Although Rózsi was raised in Austria, her mother made sure she spoke Hungarian, too. My mother and aunts didn't know Rózsi personally. They weren't allowed to go to Austria, and Rózsi couldn't come to Hungary. The borders had been closed for years. Even so, Rózsi was family, and being family, she was the first person that her Hungarian relatives contacted upon arriving in Vienna.

Soon after Blanka left, Éva left as well. She also went to Rózsi's home in Vienna. From there, she planned to follow Blanka to Canada, where she would live with one of her two older sisters. Losing Blanka and Éva was hard, especially since we knew that it would be very difficult to stay in touch. At that time, any mail that came to Hungary from the West was opened and read by the police. Naturally, our relatives were afraid to write to us. They didn't want to get us into trouble by saying the wrong thing.

My grandparents were sad to see their daughters leave, one by one. I knew they were worried that we would leave, too. My grandmother made my mother promise, over and over again, that we wouldn't go. She even made my sister and me promise! She loved us, and we loved her. We agreed—but it was a promise I feared we might not be able to keep.

Of course I didn't want to leave my grandparents or my friends or any part of my life in Magyaróvár! But all I felt inside was fear— fear of the lies I had to tell and the secrets I had to keep. More than anything, I hated the secrets.

And before long, I had another secret! In the second week of November, as my father was looking out the window one afternoon, he caught sight of two familiar women—Celia and Danielle. They were back from Budapest. They knew that it was now dangerous for us to speak, or even associate with them at all, but they had a hunch that we would look out our windows, so they stood in front of City Hall for hours! My father waited until dark and then snuck them up into our apartment. That night, the women slept at our place and left with my father at dawn. He arranged for them to be taken across the border.

In the week after Celia and Danielle left, the number of refugees passing through our town increased. It wasn't long, however, before the Soviet Union and the Kádár government started to worry that the wrong message was being sent to the world. *Hungarians wanted to get out of Hungary!* As before, the government started closing down the borders by putting up barbed-wire fences. Armed Soviet soldiers with dogs also patrolled the borders in search of refugees.

On my way to school each morning, I saw truckloads of refugees at the police station. People who had been caught at the border the previous night sat in the backs of the trucks. I felt very sorry for them, but at the same time, I was happy that *I* wasn't a captured refugee. I would *never* want any of my friends to see me sitting in one of those trucks. I would die of embarrassment!

At first, most of the refugees were let go with a warning not to try again. The ÁVOs were focused on finding freed prisoners and freedom fighters. At one point, there were so many captured refugees in our town, that the ÁVOs started holding them at the old fort while they checked their papers and figured out what should be done with them. There were not enough jail cells at the police station to hold them all. The government also introduced a strict curfew in late November. The curfew made life difficult for the refugees who had been released. They had no way of getting back to their homes and had no place to go at night!

My Uncle Laci said that the doctors at the hospital, which was across from the police station, had often allowed people to hide in the hospital basement. This gave the refugees a day or two to figure out where to go next. A few townspeople also had enough courage to break the law and take in refugees or foreigners, just as we had taken in Celia and Danielle.

Some Hungarians attempted to cross the border several times before they finally reached Austria. By December, it was very difficult to leave Hungary. To succeed, you needed two important things—a guide and a lot of money! Because the borders were now closed, you could no longer walk across to Austria in plain sight. You had to cross fields and wooded areas, and very few people knew exactly where the borders were. Many refugee guides were farmers who knew their way around the fields. Being a guide was a dangerous job, however. Getting caught meant certain death! Because of the danger, the guides charged huge amounts of money to take people to the borders. My father and another man in town helped connect people with guides. They didn't do it for money— they did it to help refugees.

Meanwhile, a debate raged in our apartment. *Should we go or should we stay?* My father loved his job, and we all loved our beautiful apartment. This was our home. And we didn't want to leave our grandparents. But how long would we be safe here? Did it even matter anymore that my father kept things running smoothly at work? The scariest thing was that my father's "secret" activities were no longer a well-kept secret!

Unfortunately, the warning signs were clear. It was time for us to leave Hungary. This realization put my mother into a state of panic. How would she break the news to my grandparents? How on earth would she decide what to pack? There were so many questions that needed answering. I can't imagine all the decisions my parents had to make before saying goodbye to their friends and family. But leaving the people they loved—knowing they might never see them again—was the hardest decision of all!

These were just a few of my parents' friends in Magyaróvár. From left to right, the arrows point to the people I recognize—my mother, my father, and Aunt Joli. The boy in the dark sailor suit is Peter Vucsics. He and his parents, Mrs. and Mr. Vucsics, were our neighbors in our apartment building.

Some captured refugees were held at the Agricultural Academy, which was once the fort. It had small windows and a river beside it, so it was difficult to escape from there.

This refugee woman and her child were caught trying to defect to Austria by crossing fields and forests. Many of the later refugees had to get to the border in the same way—by walking long distances in the dark of night.

Hungarians didn't use the word "escape"
when they talked about leaving Hungary.
Escaping would make us sound like victims,
and we weren't victims.
"We are defecting!" we said instead.
"Disszidálunk!"
I shouted this word to the world.
And in shouting, I let the world know
that we chose to leave our country.
We defected from the violence
and from the Soviet occupation.
We defected from the bondage of lies.
Fear was the enemy,
and we refused to be its victims!

Chapter Nine

Time to Go!

As my parents prepared to leave, they had to deal with another problem they hadn't anticipated—me! I had adopted a "no more secrets" policy, and now they couldn't shut me up. It was admirable, I insisted, to think and speak freely. It was admirable not to want to be afraid. I couldn't go back to denying my true feelings, but my sudden bravery had become dangerous.

I didn't stop to think that my big mouth could actually get us into trouble! For instance, my mother made the mistake of telling me that we would be leaving Hungary the next day. I wasted no time and blurted out the news to Zsuzsa, as we walked together to school.

There was a general strike in Hungary at the end of November, which meant that no one was working, and there was probably no one at school. When I rang Zsuzsa's bell, she was surprised to see me.

"Haven't you heard about the strike?" she asked. "There's no school, you know!"

But I insisted on going anyway, just in case I would see my teacher or some of my classmates. I wanted to say goodbye to everyone. Zsuzsa agreed to go with me—only because she knew it was probably our last chance to be together.

As we passed the police station, we noticed the usual truckloads of refugees being brought back from the border. Zsuzsa wondered aloud, "Will I be seeing you in one of those trucks tomorrow?"

"That's not funny!" I shouted and shot Zsuzsa a dirty look. The idea of being caught like that just mortified me! Zsuzsa knew how scared I must have been about being caught and apologized.

When we arrived at the school, we found only our teacher there. I ran into the classroom and asked her if she would miss me. She assumed I was talking about the strike.

"The strike won't last long," she said. "They'll force people back to work in no time, so don't get too used to your little holiday. You'll just have twice as much homework when you come back!"

"Not true!" I squealed. "I'm leaving Hungary tomorrow."
My teacher put her finger to her mouth. "Stop saying silly things," she warned. "You can get into trouble, you know!"

"But I won't be here to get into trouble."

My teacher shook her head in frustration. How cocky I must have seemed.

"Go home," she said finally. "Please try to keep quiet!"

It was good advice—especially after we saw announcements plastered all over buildings on our way home that said:

Zsuzsa suggested that I go to Grandmama's. She knew I felt safe there. She told me she hadn't "heard" a thing I'd said, and she hoped the teacher hadn't "heard" me, either. I hoped the teacher wouldn't report me, but I was glad I spoke out anyway! I walked Zsuzsa home and then headed over to see Tamás. Not having learned my lesson, I told Tamás my news. Then he told me his secret. His family was joining us. Tamás was coming, too!

Tamás's news made me happier than I expected. All at once, I understood how much I hadn't wanted to leave my friend. Now I just couldn't contain myself! Already the day had been a roller coaster ride of emotions, but I suppose the adventure of it all made it difficult to think—to really understand what I was feeling.

So, I didn't stop. I didn't think. Instead, I ran straight to Grandmama's house. I shouted out our plans to her—plans she was hearing for the first time. Grandmama burst into tears. In that moment, the reality of it hit me. I may never see her again! I may never see Grandpapa. I threw myself at her, hugging her tightly. Then I burst into tears, as well.

"Grandmama!" I cried. "How can I leave you?"

She pulled me down onto her lap. We both had a good cry, and she rocked me like a baby. "Don't cry for me, Babi," she said gently. But I did. I couldn't help it. I cried for her and Grandpapa. I also cried for my friend Zsuzsa, who was like a sister to me. She must feel terrible, too. There was so much to cry about, and so much to miss—my beautiful home, my beautiful town, and everyone in it that I loved!

I should be saying my goodbyes, I suddenly thought, not sitting here crying! Grandmama must have read my mind. She said, "I hope you haven't told anyone!" I shook my head, and immediately, I understood the foolishness of what I had done. Then my mother arrived. The sight of her made my grandmother start crying all over again.

"Please don't leave!" she begged. "You're my best daughter. How will I live without you?"

I suspected that she told all her daughters that they were the best. Even so, my mother was a very hard worker and she did a lot to help Grandmama. When she saw how upset her mother was, she cried as well.

"I never wanted to leave you, Mama," my mother said, sobbing. "It's just too dangerous for us *not* to leave. Imre has heard people whispering about him, and he's afraid for our lives, too."

My grandmother was sad about losing my mother, but she was also very sad about losing me. She and I loved spending time together. We planted flowers in the garden, picked fruit off the trees, and prepared delicious meals. We loved singing while we worked. Grandmama also reminded me to be thankful each day.

"You have so much to be grateful for!" she'd say. "Many people love you. I love you." To this day, I feel my grandmother's love. Even though she died long ago, her love is always with me.

I looked around Grandmama's kitchen. It was filled with the warmth of love. There was the bench beside the stove, where my sister and I sat to keep warm. An old wooden cabinet stood against one wall, its blue paint curling off. In the center of the room was the sturdy wooden kitchen table, where we ate our meals and prepared goulash and strudels. Memories of this kitchen were the inspiration for the many books I later wrote about pioneer life.

I followed Grandmama out to the yard. It was time to feed the pigs. I liked helping her with the pigs and yelled, "Soo-ey, come and get it!" before throwing their food in the pen. The pigs oinked back at me.

I tried not to get too attached to the animals in the yard and barn because I knew they would be on our table before very long. Thanks to those animals, our family never went hungry the way many other families in Hungary did under Communist rule. My grandmother often fed strangers who came to the door. She never turned away anyone who was hungry.

Everything I remember about that day is everything I loved about my grandparents. There was the cooking and the baking and the playing with the animals in the yard. These were my favorite things. For the last time, Grandpapa took Zsuzsi for a ride in the wagon and let her hold the reins. She yelled "Giddyup!" to the horses to make them go faster.

How lucky I was to have my grandparents! For nine years, they were my safe haven, and I will always be grateful for that. Now, just hours from goodbye, I wanted to cherish them. I didn't want to leave their side. I asked my mother if I could sleep at their house that night for the last time. My mother agreed, as long as I promised to stay in! She knew how much I loved my grandmother, however, and that I would never want to spend my last day in Hungary with anyone else.

This picture is of my grandmother, grandfather, and Marika, my youngest aunt. She and Aunt Joli were their only two daughters who stayed in Hungary. Marika and her husband moved to a city named Pécs soon after we left.

The friend I knew I would miss the most was Zsuzsa. She and I had known each other since we were babies. We lived in the same building and were in the same class at school. This picture was taken in front of the store that was on the first floor of our building. Zsuzsa's mother, Trudi, ran the small gas station in front of the store.

Before World War Two, the apartment building in which we lived belonged to Zsuzsa's grandparents, the Holzhammers. The Communists took it away from them. We still called the building the "Holzhammer House" while we lived there. Zsuzsa's grandfather's name is on the store sign in this old photo.

When you see the face of the enemy up close,

you realize the enemy isn't a person.

The enemy is the fear that drives

a person to hurt others.

How hard it must be to hurt others for an idea!

I looked into the faces of the soldiers,

and I saw two young boys—boys who would

rather be home with their families.

Like us, they liked to play and laugh,

but, instead, they were ordered to kill.

I wonder if those boys talk about

the fun we had that night.

I wonder...

Do they still play the game I taught them?

Chapter Ten

Back so Soon?

It was Thursday, November 29th, the day before my father's 35th birthday. We would celebrate his last birthday in Hungary that evening. As night approached, however, we felt less and less like celebrating. But Grandmama cooked us a delicious dinner, and Marika and Miklós came to share it with us. We figured it would be our last meal together because we planned to leave Hungary the next afternoon.

My other grandmother, Grandmama Rózsi, lived in Szeged, which was in the south of Hungary. She had no idea what was going on with us. There was no way my father could call her or even send a letter. My father's brother Béla knew nothing of our plans, either. He also lived in Szeged, so it was comforting for my father to know that his mother wouldn't be left alone. My father didn't cry often, but he was very upset that night. We were all crying. I'm sure it was a birthday celebration he never forgot!

Although we reassured one another that we'd be together soon, Grandmama knew differently. After all, she hadn't seen her two oldest daughters in many years and had never even met nine of her grandchildren. Sadly, she'd come to accept their absence, but she had recently lost two more daughters, Blanka and Éva. She hoped they were safe in Austria or Canada now. We hadn't heard a word from either one. Now, Grandmama also had to deal with losing us. We would all suffer from losing one another!

The next day, we came home from Grandmama's house early and got ready for our journey. Our bags were packed. We each had two huge suitcases to carry. My father was in charge of the cars at the Kühne factory, so he had arranged for a driver to pick us up. Very few people in Hungary owned cars, and most weren't even allowed to drive them. We were lucky! The driver had agreed to take us to a place near the Hegyeshalom border, which was not far from our home. It would require two trips to drive all seven of us. My mother, Zsuzsi, Tamás, his mother, and I would be in the first carload. We would wait at a house until the driver drove back to pick up my father and Tamás's father. Then we would cross the border from there.

Not only did our suitcases fill the trunk of the car, they were piled onto its roof, as well. We secured the luggage with ropes, but what a sight! We might as well have put a neon sign on the car, advertising "defectors inside!"

Hoping that no one would notice the obvious, we drove out of Magyaróvár. The roads were empty, but, in no time, we saw a police car behind us. It passed our car and then cut us off. Our driver stopped. Both he and a police officer got out of their cars.

They talked briefly, and our driver returned. Then we were off—only this time, we were tailing the police! They led us to the border barracks, where the officers ordered us out of our car.

A border guard took each of our mothers into a different room. Our mothers were separated so they couldn't corroborate, or agree upon, their stories. Zsuzsi, Tamás, and I got to stick together and were put into another room. In our room, however, sat two Soviet soldiers with guns. When we walked in, the soldiers pointed their guns at us and laughed.

In broken Hungarian, they introduced themselves. Their names were Vlad and Yuri. Vlad and Yuri looked like kids. In fact, they hardly looked older than sixteen. And they weren't mean, as I expected. Almost at once, Yuri pulled a picture out of his pocket. It was of a young girl my age—a girl he said was his sister. I'd never thought of Soviets as having sisters. Soviets were the faceless enemy I had learned to hate.

Vlad and Yuri were in the middle of a card game. I pointed to the cards and then to us to show that we wanted to play, too. I told my sister and Tamás that I planned to teach them Gypsy Rummy, a card game that could take hours to play. My sister immediately started screaming at me.

"You're going to get us killed! You're such a cheater. And if you win the game, they'll shoot us!"

The soldiers couldn't understand what my sister was saying, but they were curious. Why was my sister so upset? They pointed a gun at the deck of cards.

"Play!" they shouted in Hungarian. We did as we were told.

I dealt out the cards and started laying down my first "creative" hand. My only rule with this game was that I made up the rules as I went along. The soldiers scratched their heads in confusion. They were clearly trying to follow what I was doing. I just smiled and laid out hand after hand. Tamás tried to keep up with me, but he had never beaten me in his life. Zsuzsi refused to play and just kept muttering that I would get us all killed. Every once in a while, I allowed the soldiers to gain some points. It was like taking candy from a baby. They were intrigued by my complicated game and were determined to beat me!

While our card game was going on, I heard a familiar voice in the hallway. It was my father's voice. He must have been just outside the room where we were being held. I found out that the police brought him and Tamás's father to the barracks to be interrogated, as well. He asked the police if he could talk to us first and then have his driver take us home. He told them to hold him responsible and to let the rest of us go. The police agreed to let us kids go, but our mothers had to stay.

When my father came into the room and saw I was playing Gypsy Rummy with the soldiers, he shook his head and laughed.

"I'm amazed they didn't shoot you, Babi. I've often been tempted to shoot you when you've played that game with me!"

The soldiers seemed to understand what was going on and winked at me before saying goodbye. After that card game, I could never understand why people were afraid of the Soviets!

The driver first took Tamás home to his grandparents and then drove us to our grandparents' house. I couldn't wait to tell Grandmama about beating the Soviet soldiers at cards. It was after eleven o'clock when we arrived, however. My grandparents had been asleep and were very frightened to hear a car stop in front of their home. They sensed that something had gone terribly wrong! We told them that Mom and Dad were being held at the border barracks by the police and that they would go home to the apartment after they were released.

Grandmama promptly put us to bed. Before I fell asleep, I told her how much fun I had with the Soviet soldiers and that one of the soldiers had a sister my age.

"All people are good," she said. "It's just that sometimes they do bad things."

"I don't think those Soviets want to do bad things. I don't think they want to hurt Hungarians at all."

"You're probably right, Babi. But they're also afraid not to follow orders."

"Fear," my grandmother said, as she gently tucked me in, "is the biggest enemy we have."

My parents went home to our apartment about two hours after we reached our grandparents' house. They didn't come to see us that night, but my mother *did* come to see us the next morning. She told Zsuzsi and me very little about what had happened at the barracks. Perhaps she suspected that I could no longer keep a secret. All she said to me was, "Dad's had better birthdays!"

I *did* overhear Mom telling my grandmother, however, that she and Tamás's mother, Aunt Ica, were questioned in separate rooms. When the guards asked them where they were going in the car, they came up with different stories. Mom said we were going to visit relatives in one town, and Aunt Ica mentioned another town. My father and Tamás's father, Uncle János, finally told the truth. The guards warned our parents that it was against the law to leave the country, and if they tried again they'd be put in jail. Of course, our fathers promised to stay in Hungary!

"But we're going to try again," my mother whispered to my grandmother. "Tomorrow!"

I wasn't surprised to hear this news, but it scared me. We knew the ÁVOs would be watching our every move from now on. My mother actually went food shopping that morning, just to make it look as though we were, indeed, staying!

Zsuzsa's mother, Trudi, almost fainted when she saw my mother standing in line for milk early that morning. In Hungary, you couldn't just buy food at a grocery store. You had to line up for hours for milk or bread or meat—all at different shops. Trudi said nothing to my mother at the store, but she later invited her up for tea. Apparently, when Zsuzsa's family heard the floorboards creaking above them in the middle of the night, they thought the ÁVOs had come to claim our apartment! In the safety of Trudi's home, my mother finally told her the story. She also confessed that we were leaving again the next day, and this time, we had to do it the hard way—on foot.

Before my mother left Grandmama's house that morning, she gave me strict orders not to leave the house. She made me promise not to talk to anyone about the night before. It never occurred to me then that my big mouth *may* have caused our capture! I promised, but I didn't keep my promise for very long.

When my friend Mari came to see me a few hours later, I just *had* to tell her about my card game with the soldiers! How could a person keep such juicy news to herself? Mari said I was very brave to play my game with the Soviets. She then asked me if my family would try to defect again. I knew what was at stake this time, and I said "No!" I told her I'd see her at school on Monday.

Soon after Mari left, someone else arrived. It was my Aunt Joli from Budapest! We hadn't heard a word from her since the Revolution, and we were very worried about her and her family. I squealed with delight when I saw my two baby cousins. While I played with the girls, Grandpapa asked Joli where her husband János was. I then heard Joli tell her story to my grandparents.

"After the Soviet tanks came in on November 4th, the fighting started again in Budapest. The tanks blew huge holes into the sides of buildings, so I was afraid to stay in our apartment. The girls and I stayed in the basement of our building while János fought in the streets. Before long, we knew we were fighting a losing battle and that János had to leave. The ÁVOs had arrested many of the freedom fighters and were hanging them. János and I decided that the best way for him to get out of Hungary was to pretend he and I were visiting family in Magyaróvár.

"János and I went to the train station together. I showed my birth certificate to the police to prove where I was born and said we were going home for a visit. We both boarded the train, but then I got off. Before I left the train, János casually asked me to hide his two guns. I didn't even know he had guns in the apartment!

"I was scared out of my mind," Joli said, "because I knew that anyone caught with a weapon was hanged! I was also furious that János had left guns in our apartment. So, in the middle of the night, I put the guns into a bucket and carried the bucket to the basement. I didn't think anyone would suspect anything! People constantly carry buckets to the basement to get sawdust to heat their apartments.

"Using a small shovel, I dug a hole in the dirt floor and put the bucket containing the guns into it. I then filled the bucket with dirt and covered the hole." Joli shook her head.

"I told no one that I did this, but the very next evening, two ÁVOs appeared at my door with the guns! I claimed to know nothing about them. I couldn't imagine who could have seen what I'd done or would actually report me! When the ÁVOs couldn't get me to admit anything, they asked where János was. I told them my husband had run off with another woman."

She laughed at her own cunning. "I told them I never wanted to see him again! I then asked the ÁVOs to come in and see my baby girls.

"'Their father left them, too,' I cried. 'I have no choice now but to go to Magyaróvár and live with my parents.'

"When the ÁVOs looked at my two adorable babies, they smiled and wished me good luck. It took me a couple of weeks to pack what I needed and sell our other belongings. I hoped that János was waiting for us here so we could leave Hungary together."

But János hadn't come to see my grandparents. We later found out that he'd bumped into my father in town and asked him not to tell the family that he was leaving. Being a freedom fighter, he knew that the fewer people who knew about his whereabouts and plans, the less likely that he would get caught and arrested.

When I heard Joli's story, I wanted desperately to tell ours. I told her how we'd been caught the night before, trying to defect. Of course, I also told her that we were leaving again the next day. Before I even finished my sentence, Joli got very excited and said,

"I'm coming with you!"

Just then, my father walked into the house and overheard our conversation.

"You can't possibly cross the border with two babies!" he said. "If we're caught again, I'll go to jail, and Vali and the children will suffer, too. I'm sorry, Joli, but we can't take any more chances."

"I'll stay with Joli," I offered. "I'll look after my little cousins. Grandmama needs me, and now Joli needs me, too!"

My father looked at me and smiled. "After your card game last night, Babi, I hear the whole Soviet army is looking for you! Do you really want to face their wrath?"

I wasn't sure if my father was kidding, but I thought I should probably leave Hungary with my parents after all!

Which took more courage—to stay or to leave?

Each choice was as hard as the other.

To stay meant probable imprisonment for my father

and a hard life for our family.

To leave was just as difficult.

It meant leaving behind everything we owned.

It meant leaving behind the people we loved.

It meant going forward with nothing.

To stay or to leave?

Both required incredible courage!

Chapter Eleven

The Final Farewell

It was Sunday, December 2nd. We all attended church that morning to pray for a safe crossing into Austria. We then went to my grandparents' house for lunch. Our last few hours with my grandparents, aunts, and cousins were happy. We had already said our tearful goodbyes the first time we left. Today, for the second time, we kissed our relatives goodbye. We then returned to our apartment.

"Girls, I think we should all take a nap," my mother said. "We'll probably have to walk the whole night."

We agreed and even lay down on our beds, but none of us could sleep. We were leaving in about three hours. Leaving this time felt very different. It wasn't as exciting as it was the first time. It was frightening! We knew that we had to succeed or, as the government posters said, face "dire consequences."

As I was getting dressed to leave, I took a look around our apartment. I knew we'd never be back. I tried to memorize all our furniture, my clothes, and each one of my toys. All these things were hard to obtain in Hungary, and they were very hard to leave behind! We were grateful to own even the smallest items, and, as a result, each one of them was special.

My mother packed just a couple of treasured pieces of art. I packed my doll. We wore as many layers of clothing as we could. "If we can *wear* it," we joked, "we don't have to *carry* it." We didn't want to arouse suspicion this time by carrying heavy suitcases. Finally, it was time to go. Just one more thing I had to do. I reached under my bed and pulled out my Lenin book. I put it into a ceramic stove. I don't know if it was ever burned or not, but I had no further use for it in my life.

We took one final look around and, with heavy hearts, closed the door of our apartment for the last time. I had tears in my eyes, but a voice in my head said, *Don't look back, just keep on walking!* I did. We headed down the stairs to Lenin Street. We hoped we wouldn't see anyone we knew on our way to the bus.

But, of course, we did! In the distance, we saw Zsuzsa and her mother Trudi coming toward us. I wanted to hug my friend goodbye and tell her that I would write, but Trudi wouldn't allow her to come near me. She knew a tearful goodbye was the last thing we needed right now. I waved to Zsuzsa, and she waved back. We looked right into each other's eyes. *I'm losing one of my closest friends*, I thought, and I know that Zsuzsa thought it, too.

Thankfully, we passed no other friends or acquaintances. We reached the bus stop and waited patiently. Within minutes, the Nagy family arrived. Because of my "no more secrets policy," no one had told me that Tamás and his family were coming with us again. To be safe, we didn't speak with them, but Tamás looked at Zsuzsi and me and smiled. It felt good to know that one of our best friends was coming with us.

There were many strangers waiting for the bus. We knew they must be defectors because they were very subdued. Travelers weren't usually this quiet. Like us, many of them were heading to the village of Rajka. Rajka was at the intersection of Austria, Czechoslovakia, and Hungary. The border at Rajka was riskier to cross than the borders at Hegyeshalom or Sopron were. At the Rajka crossing, it was easy for refugees to make a wrong turn and enter Czechoslovakia, which was also occupied by the Soviet Union. Under orders from the Soviets, the Czechoslovakian people had to turn over all refugees to the Hungarian border guards.

We boarded the bus when it arrived, but we didn't sit near Tamás and his parents. Our two families got off before everyone else did, however. We had not yet reached Rajka. In minutes, another bus came along and picked us up. This second bus was empty. When we got on, the driver instructed each of us to take a separate seat. We were to lie, rather than sit, so that the backs of the seats would hide us.

We didn't get more than five minutes down Rajka Road before some Hungarian soldiers stopped us. Our driver promptly opened the door, and a soldier walked up the two steps of the bus. He took a quick look and left again. Our hearts were in our throats! Why didn't the soldier check the bus more thoroughly? And why wasn't our driver worried? We decided that he might have given the soldier some money. People made a lot of money helping defectors. It cost us almost our *entire* savings to leave Hungary!

Eventually, the driver turned onto a country road. The bus slowed to a stop at the end of this road, and we got off. It was around six o'clock and, being December, it was already dark. The driver pointed to a farmhouse surrounded by fields and woods. Cautiously, we walked for about five minutes in the direction of lights that shone from the windows of the house.

We knocked at the door, and a man told us to enter. He motioned for us to sit at the large kitchen table. Sitting across from us were two men who were refugees from Budapest and who would be crossing the border with us. They offered to help us because they needed more money to pay the guides. My father made a deal with them that if they helped carry our bags, he would give the guides extra money on their behalf.

There was a woman in the kitchen, too. She was cooking a pot of bean soup with ham. The heat of the stove made the kitchen feel cozy, and the smell of the soup made our mouths water. The woman's husband was one of our guides. Their neighbor was our other guide. The woman told us to take off our coats. She gave us each a steaming bowl of the soup and a slice of fresh bread. We were very hungry, as well as cold, so we were happy to have the hot food. Neither the woman, the guides, nor the two men from Budapest told us their names. Not knowing one another's names was a precaution. If anything went wrong, we wouldn't be able to identify the others, and they couldn't identify us, either.

The guides told us that we would be heading out at about ten o'clock, so they urged us to get some sleep in another room. This room was drafty and cold. We put on our coats to keep warm. The beds in the room were made of wood, and a rope netting supported the lumpy straw mattresses. Zsuzsi, Tamás, and I had to share a bed. To fit, we lay down on it sideways.

The minute we lay down, we started to giggle. Our giggling annoyed the adults, but how could we help it? When one of us looked at another, the giggles started. We knew we had nothing to laugh about, but we couldn't stop. We giggled because we were scared to death! We got no sleep at all, of course. Ten o'clock came quickly, and it was time to leave the house. Before we left, we received strict warnings from all the adults.

The guides told us that if we didn't behave ourselves, we would surely be killed by the Soviets! They then informed us about the journey ahead. The first challenge, they said, would be to cross Rajka Road. They were very worried about crossing this main road because there was a full moon. The border guards kept their eyes on the road, and the bright sky meant it would be easier for them to spot us as we crossed it. The guides kept telling us that the moonlight would fade, but it seemed only to get brighter!

Before we reached the road, we had to go through a wooded area. We could hear dogs barking in the distance. The sound alerted us to the fact that danger surrounded us. Moving from one tree to the next, we inched our way closer to Rajka Road. Finally, we were at the edge of the woods. While we hid in the woods, we clung to the trees for support. From behind my tree, I stole a glance at the road. It was snowing, but only enough to moisten the ground. Then more snow fell. I couldn't help thinking what a beautiful night it was!

But we were still at the start of our journey, not far from the farmhouse. We had miles of wooded areas and fields to cross, and these were on the other side of the road. After three hours of hugging trees, my father couldn't take it anymore! He suggested that we cross the road on our hands and knees, staying as low as possible. We started out one at a time, crawling and pulling our bags across the snow-covered pavement. Soon, we were all on the other side. It was already two in the morning, and we worried that we wouldn't reach the Austrian border before daybreak.

We hugged our trees and used them to hide and support us while we waited in the woods for the moonlight to fade. But the moon seemed only to get brighter and brighter. My sister is on the left of a tree, and I am on the right. Our parents are behind us. Tamás and his family are hiding behind another tree.

As we walked and walked, our feet got heavier. Pounds of mud and snow stuck to the soles of our boots, but we couldn't give up. We still had a long way to go. Across the Czechoslovakian border, soldiers were shooting flares into the sky every few minutes to help the Hungarian border guards spot defectors. Each time a flare went up, a burst of light brightened the sky, and we had to dive to the ground. We had to lie flat so we wouldn't be seen by the border guards. After a while, all this getting up and dropping down made my legs feel as heavy as lead.

Still, we had a long journey ahead. We walked for at least two more hours before we came to a large stream. When I saw the knee-deep water, I started to cry. Nobody could make me go in there! Already, I was shivering and the water looked freezing. My father offered to pay the guides extra money to carry us all across. Tamás was still recovering from rheumatic fever, so it was especially important for him not to go into the cold water.

The two refugee men took our bags and came back to carry us. One by one, they and the guides took our families across, starting with us children. When I was safely on the other side, I watched one of the men piggyback my father. My father was a big man. I hoped he and the guide wouldn't both fall into the water!

We *must* be near the Austrian border, I thought. When I found out that we were actually closer to the Czechoslovakian border, I started to cry out loud. I didn't think I could walk another step! The next time a flare went up, I dropped down and refused to get up. My father tried to reason with me, but I wouldn't budge.

"Leave!" I commanded. "I told you that I wanted to stay with Aunt Joli and the girls. Go without me! The guards will find me and take me back to Grandmama's. I'll be fine!"

My father was exhausted, too, but he leaned over and plucked me out of the mud. He carried me for about five minutes before reminding me that I was the oldest, and I had to be brave. Neither my sister nor Tamás had to be carried! Of course, this shamed me into walking again. It even gave me a small burst of energy. The energy didn't last long, but it didn't matter. Soon the guides told us that we were close to the Austrian border. Close enough, they said, to finish the journey without them. They gestured to some lights in the distance.

"That's an Austrian village," they said. But how faint the lights were! We could also make out the faint lights of Czechoslovakia, so, at times, it was hard to know which lights we were supposed to be following!

All we could do was keep walking! We walked for about another hour, in what we hoped was the right direction. Then, without warning, we heard the most beautiful sound…

"Hier!" we heard someone shout in the darkness. *"Schnell! Kommen Sie hier, bitte,"* which meant, "Here! Quick! Come here, please." On hearing the German language, we knew it had to be an Austrian border guard. He was shouting at us to come toward him and not to walk toward Czechoslovakia.

Austrian border guards were not allowed to cross the border to rescue refugees who were in danger, but they often yelled out to let them know where Austria was. At this border crossing, it would have been easy for us to enter Czechoslovakia by mistake. We also heard stories about refugees who crossed the border, got confused, and walked back into Hungary. There were no markers to show the way, and the guides didn't go all the way to the border.

Flares were being fired more frequently now, and the sky was constantly lit up. The dogs of the Hungarian border guards were barking more loudly, as well. Although the guards may not have seen us, they knew that some refugees were trying to escape. They shot a hail of bullets into the sky as a warning—or perhaps they were shooting someone! On hearing the gunfire, my dad shouted, "Run as fast as you can! Drop whatever you can't carry."

My sister, Tamás, and I dropped our suitcases. We were so tired, we weren't sure we could make it, even without them. We ran as fast as our legs would carry us, but Tamás started to fall far behind the rest of us. Because of his recent illness, he wasn't supposed to run at all, and he was having trouble breathing.

Seeing that Tamás was in trouble, his father dropped his suitcase, turned around, and picked him up. He ran with Tamás in his arms. My father grabbed Uncle János's suitcase and carried it along with his own.

The distance we had to run should have taken minutes, but it seemed like an eternity! My fear amplified the sound of the barking dogs, and my heart was in my throat. I couldn't breathe. When I cried out again that I couldn't make it, my father shouted, "Run, Babi, because you want to live. Run because you want to be free!" He was panting, trying to encourage me while he was running for *his* life. It was a moment I'll never forget. I faced my fear and found the strength to live. I ran to save my life. One after the other, we all made it across the border.

The guards greeted us with, "Good Morning. Welcome to Austria!" As they came to shake our hands, we jumped up and down and shouted "Thank you!" as loud as we could. The men and Tamás shook hands with the guards, and our mothers hugged them. Zsuzsi and I gave them kisses on their cheeks.

The guards smiled and pointed at our clothes. We were muddy from head to toe from hitting the dirt so many times. Speaking of hitting the dirt, my mother suddenly shouted, "Everybody down!" We were so used to doing this, that we dropped to the ground without thinking. "It's time to kiss the Austrian soil," she said. "We're free at last!" So, we all laughed and kissed the soil. Freedom tasted wonderful!

After our soil-kissing ritual, the border guards pointed us in the direction of the village of Nickelsdorf, which was not too far from where we were. They told us to go to the school there. Within minutes, we found it. A woman who spoke Hungarian met us at the door. Because this village was so close to Hungary, many people there had Hungarian parents or had once lived in Hungary. The woman asked us to follow her. The town was still asleep, but the school was open for refugees, who poured in nightly.

By the time we arrived in Austria, about 150,000 refugees had already left Hungary through various border crossings. Most of the other border areas were now almost impossible to cross, so many of the refugees who came after us also crossed at the Rajka-Nickelsdorf border.

A couple of women from the village brought coffee and tea for us to drink. We were shivering, but we felt much better after we had a hot drink. Our shoes and clothes were muddy, so one of the women took us outside to show us where we could pump water from a well and wash off our boots. They gave us rags for wiping the mud from our clothes. We did our best to clean up, one after the other, using the cold well water in freezing December weather.

After we came inside, we sat on the floor of the school, along with the other refugees. My mother showed one of the Austrian women my aunt Rózsi's address in Vienna and asked how we could get there. The woman said a train would take us there later. In the meantime, she suggested we get some sleep. There was straw on the floor to make sitting and sleeping more comfortable. We took off our filthy clothes, and Zsuzsi and I put on new track suits, which my mother had packed in her suitcase. I was happy that we hadn't packed them in our suitcases!

It was then that I remembered what was in the bag that I'd thrown away. I had packed my doll in that bag! I wondered if I could sneak back across the border to get it. When I was sure my parents were asleep, I headed toward the border to look for my bag. I knew that it couldn't be very far, and I would probably find it easily, now that it was light outside. As I ran across the field, I spotted the bag right away.

When I bent over to pick it up, I noticed a Soviet soldier's boot stepping on the handle. The soldier's dog had its nose inside the bag and was sniffing at my doll. I grabbed the doll quickly and started to run. The soldier shot bullets into the air and screamed at me to stop. Suddenly, the Austrian guards, my parents, and my grandparents appeared and were all screaming at me.

"You silly girl! You had your freedom. Why did you go back?"

"I couldn't leave my doll behind!" I cried.

"You'll never be free now," they said and then disappeared.

Why did I go back? I questioned myself over and over, crying. *I was safe. I had kissed the soil of freedom!*

At that moment, my mother woke me up. I had been crying and shaking in my sleep. She held me and rocked me in her arms. "You had a bad dream, my Babi! Try to get some sleep."

When I woke up, I realized that I was safe in Austria. For the next 25 years, however, I had that same nightmare. Almost every night, I crossed the border in my sleep to rescue my doll.

The greatest power we possess

is the power to tell the truth.

I never thought about who I really was

until the Revolution happened.

Then I started making choices for myself.

Each difficult moment

opened my eyes and my heart.

I became aware of my goodness and strength.

I became aware of my dreams.

My dreams became my truths.

Chapter Twelve

We Are Now Refugees

Later that day, we caught the train to Vienna. On the train, I sat by a window. The bleak December landscape passing by hypnotized me, and my mind started to wander. When the conductor came around and asked to see our tickets, he realized that we had no tickets.

"*Ach, Flüchtlinge!*" he said in German. "Ah, refugees." He nodded and allowed us to travel for free to Vienna. The word "refugee" echoed in my mind.

I suddenly realized that it was official—we were refugees. Refugees are people who seek refuge from a dangerous situation. A refuge is a safe shelter. We were finally in Austria, which was a safe place where the ÁVOs couldn't find us or beat up our fathers or tell us what to think or say anymore. It was a place where we could sing the Hungarian anthem and truly be Hungarian. We weren't allowed to be Hungarian in Hungary. We were supposed to forget that our country had a history before the Soviet Union took it over. We were told to forget our culture and traditions.

Being a refugee meant I had no home and no possessions. I had only my family and myself. It meant I had to leave the past behind because I couldn't go back there anymore. I didn't know what my future would be, so I couldn't think about that, either. So, there was only one thing left to do—enjoy my life right now.

Everything I had ever known about Austria was right out of fairy tales. I had heard that there were many castles in Vienna and that kings, queens, and princesses lived there a long time ago. They were just like the people in my fairy tales. I imagined what it would be like to be a princess. Then I thought, *I could be a princess right now.* What if people recognized me as royalty and treated me with love and kindness? What if my time in Vienna became my very own fairy tale? *Hmmm,* I mused. *Why not? Why can't I live the life of my dreams right here and right now?* Celia had told me to dream big and to believe in my dreams.

"What are you thinking about, Babi?" my father asked.

"I was just wondering. Who am I? Who am I right now?"

"Oh Babi," he said. "Just another one of your simple questions. You're quite the philosopher, aren't you?"

I didn't know what a philosopher was, but I figured it was a person who liked to think. I thought about all kinds of things. I created different worlds in my mind. One minute, I was Kálmán Babi the Booklover, and the next, I was Kálmán Babi the Princess. Today, I was Kálmán Babi the homeless, sleepless, secretless, fearless, and very powerful refugee! Today, I could accomplish *anything* I wanted to accomplish because I had nothing to lose.

"So," my father asked, "have you decided who you are?"

I smiled happily. "Yes I have," I said. "I'm anything I want to be—and I want to be everything!"

"I have no doubt, Babi, that nothing will stop you! But do you think you could get off the train with the rest of us now?"

We got off the train in Vienna and found Aunt Rózsi's apartment with help from a friendly policeman. It was now past six o'clock in the evening, but Aunt Rózsi wasn't home yet. She had no idea that we were even in Austria—let alone at her home! We made ourselves comfortable on the floor of her hallway, thinking she'd be home at any moment. When one of the neighbors came out to see why seven people were sitting on the floor, we pointed to Rózsi's door.

"Ah, refugees!" she remarked in German.

"I'm Rózsi's cousin," my mother answered, also in German.

The woman's son was very curious about us and peeked out into the hallway to have a look. He asked his mother if we could come in. She nodded and motioned for us to enter her apartment. The woman must have guessed that we were hungry because she went into the kitchen and soon brought out sandwiches for everyone. She also made tea for the adults and gave us kids milk to drink. This was our introduction to the people of Vienna. In the two months we lived there, not a *single* person was unkind to us!

At nine o'clock, Aunt Rózsi came home. When the neighbor heard her unlock her door, she went out into the hallway and told Aunt Rózsi that there were some refugees in her apartment.

Aunt Rózsi had taken Blanka and Éva into her home a few weeks before, but she didn't know how she could house seven people in a one-bedroom apartment! It was too late to find us another place to stay, so she started to panic. Her neighbor offered to take us children and asked another neighbor to allow Tamás's parents to sleep at their place. My parents slept at Aunt Rózsi's.

We understood why our aunt felt panicked, having so many strangers show up at her door. Even my mother was a stranger. Hungarians couldn't cross the border into Austria, so Rózsi and my mother had met only once, as children.

None of us slept well that night. We were overtired from our walk across the border and worried about where we would live. In the morning, the neighbor suggested that our parents leave us children there for the day so our mothers could go out and get "gray cards," or travel passes. Travel passes allowed us to use Vienna's public transportation for free. Aunt Rózsi asked her fiancé Karl, a policeman, to help our fathers find us a place to stay.

While our parents were out, Zsuzsi, Tamás, and I played with the neighbor's son. The boy gave us some bubble gum. We'd never seen bubble gum before, so when he showed us how to blow bubbles, we encountered some serious problems! Zsuzsi learned how to blow huge bubbles right away and started teasing Tamás because he kept blowing the wad of gum clear out of his mouth.

When Zsuzsi blew another bubble, Tamás grabbed it and yanked the gum right out of her mouth. Zsuzsi was furious! The next time Tamás sent his gum flying out of *his* mouth, she grabbed

it and slapped it against his backside. None of us knew that gum was sticky, and we were surprised when it stuck to Tamás's pants. Tamás was still holding Zsuzsi's gum, so he smacked her in the head with it. By now, they'd figured out just how sticky the gum was, and knew they were in BIG TROUBLE! The boy's mother tried to get the gum off Tamás's pants, but most of it was still stuck. Zsuzsi's hair was even worse. The gum was now lodged in a big clump of her hair.

Our mothers returned tired and irritable. They'd been standing in line for hours, waiting to get travel passes, and they hadn't slept for the last two nights. The gum fight was the straw that broke the camel's back. Both our mothers were furious! Tamás's mother tried to scrape the gum carefully off his pants with a razor blade. My mother asked Aunt Rózsi for some scissors and snipped off a chunk of Zsuzsi's hair. Both kids were told to face the wall and not say a word to each other. I also didn't say a word, knowing it wouldn't take much to trigger my mother's temper!

Uncle Karl and our fathers returned before very long. They had found a shelter where we could stay the night. We thanked Aunt Rózsi and her neighbors and grabbed our bags. We were all exhausted! Uncle Karl took us to the shelter. He told my father that there were many relief offices all over Vienna where refugees could get vouchers for clothes and meals, as well as for places to stay. Uncle Karl was sorry he hadn't been able to find us a good place that day and suggested our fathers go to some relief offices in the morning to find a better refugee shelter.

The refugee shelter was a big barn. We had to sleep on platforms covered with straw mattresses. My sister and I slept next to some people we'd never met before. Our parents slept on the platform below us. Tamás and his family were on yet another platform. We got very little sleep again, for the third night in a row.

My father and Uncle János woke up early the next morning and lined up at the first relief office they could find. They couldn't believe who was working there—it was Celia! Celia had been very worried about us. After leaving Magyaróvár, she'd heard only bad news about Hungary and wasn't able to find out if we were safe. She actually stayed in Vienna, hoping we would leave Hungary!

When my father appeared at the office, Celia was in shock! She let out a loud cry and then hugged my father for several minutes. Dad told her about our difficult border crossing and about where we were now living. She immediately found us a great place to stay—a cooking school in Old Vienna.

This old picture shows part of Old Vienna, the most beautiful area of the city.

The cooking school was run by Catholic nuns. Men were not allowed to sleep at the school, but they could visit and eat there during the day. My father and Uncle János would be sleeping at a church, but they didn't care where they slept, as long as their wives and children were safe and comfortable.

Celia took us all to the cooking school first and said she would take our fathers to the church later. While we settled in, she told us about the refugee situation in Vienna. She said that 70,000 refugees had already left Austria for other countries, but 80,000 were still there, and more were arriving each day.

Celia also shared some happy news with us. While in Vienna, she had fallen in love with an American university professor. She felt that we were responsible for her happiness! After we'd helped her in Hungary, she wanted to repay our family by helping Hungarian refugees in Vienna. She planned to stay in Austria for a while longer and then go to the United States to get married.

Celia's student Danielle was now back in Paris. Celia told us that she would send her a telegram to let her know that we were safe in Vienna. In less than a week, Danielle's family sent us money. We used the money to buy food and clothes when we arrived in our new home.

I was amazed by the series of events that were taking place in our lives! First we helped Celia, and Celia felt so grateful that she wanted to help others. Then just when we really needed someone to give us a hand, Celia showed up in our lives once again. Who was waiting for us around the next corner?

When you have nothing,

you learn to receive from others.

Someone will always take care of you,

if you trust and reach out your hand.

When you have nothing,

everything is a miracle.

Just look around you,

and enjoy life's simple pleasures.

They are everywhere.

When you have nothing,

you are free to discover everything!

Chapter Thirteen

Wonderful Vienna

We were delighted to be living at the cooking school. It was very comfortable, and we felt safe there. Although Vienna was not a dangerous city, we had just experienced a revolution and a scary border crossing, so it was still hard for us to feel safe. We needed to be able to relax and get some sleep!

At the cooking school, about 30 women and children slept in a big room on air mattresses, the kind you see in swimming pools. We shared one bathroom, which our fathers also used during the day, so having a bath was definitely a challenge.

Each night at the school was like a pajama party. The women and children who lived with us became our friends, and we had fun together. We put on funny skits to entertain one another. The greatest joy of living at the school, however, was the food! We were offered dishes we had never eaten before. I loved the spices used by the Austrians. I especially loved the wonderful pastries. Austrian desserts were delicious—and Austrians put whipped cream on almost everything. I was sure I was in heaven!

Old Vienna, where the cooking school was located, had the most beautiful architecture! Sometimes we walked around the center of the city all day, just looking at the magnificent buildings, such as churches and palaces, which had been there for hundreds of years. Being December, the city sparkled with Christmas lights and decorations.

My mother loved walking down Mariahilfer Street, where there were many cafés and shops with decorated Christmas windows. I had never seen such luxuries. There were no shops like that in Hungary, and we certainly had no Christmas windows filled with wonderful toys! A huge Christmas tree stood in front of City Hall, and all around it, the biggest *Christkindlmarkt* in Vienna bustled with activity.

Vienna sparkled with lights. In front of City Hall was a huge Christmas market.

A *Christkindlmarkt* is a Christmas market, where gifts are sold. We walked through it and saw all kinds of toys. Some of the booths also sold food and *Glühwein*, a hot, spiced wine. Celia had given my parents some money, so they bought themselves a cup of *Glühwein* each and treated us to hot chocolate and roasted chestnuts. We had very little money, but we didn't need much. Seeing beautiful Vienna was the best holiday we'd ever had!

But we didn't just make our own fun. In the weeks leading up to Christmas, the Austrians gathered refugee children from various camps and shelters almost daily and treated us to parties and gifts. Sometimes they took us to department stores and encouraged us to pick out clothes. At other times, they gave us food, candy, or toys. We were even taken out at night. Our parents came with us on these special occasions.

One evening, a Bishop invited us to dine with him. He welcomed us to Austria and talked to us about the huge changes we were experiencing in our lives. He reminded us that if we kept our faith, we would be taken care of on the difficult journey ahead. This statement surprised us kids. Our parents may have been focused on the future, but we kids were having the time of our lives in Vienna! Every day there felt like Christmas.

About two weeks before Christmas, the nuns at the cooking school told us that we'd be going to a Christmas play put on for us by some children, whose parents were members of the Gymnastics and Sports Club of Kaisermühlen. Kaisermühlen was a district of Vienna. Hundreds of Hungarian children were invited to the play.

(above) The Bishop's party was held at a hotel. I am on the extreme left, Tamás is beside me, and Zsuzsi is behind him. The Bishop greeted each one of us. (below) Hundreds of children were invited to the Christmas play at the sports club. We were very excited and happy to be there.

Zsuzsi and me

When we arrived at the play, we were seated at long wooden tables. We finally settled down in our seats, and the play began. A beautiful girl, dressed in a long, blue, silky robe, stood in the center of the stage. She was playing Mary, Jesus' mother. The spotlight was on her, but she was also illuminated by a light that shone from within her. She was more like an angel than a child. A makeshift manger was at her feet, in which lay a doll that I knew right away was supposed to be baby Jesus.

I'd never before seen such a wonderful doll! All I could think of was holding it in my arms. I stared at this "baby Jesus" and imagined what it would be like to have such a doll. I couldn't take my eyes off it. I missed the doll that I lost at the Austrian border and was still having nightmares about going back for it.

At the end of the play, the organizers of the party announced a surprise. The club members had offered to take the children who were at the play into their homes over the Christmas holidays. I wasn't sure I liked the idea because I worried about leaving my parents. I also worried about not being able to speak German. How would we communicate?

It took a while for the names to be called, but when my sister and I were chosen to live with a certain family, I knew a miracle had occurred! We were going to be living in the home of the girl who played Mary, and she owned the baby Jesus doll. Her name was Elfi. The fact that Mr. Hans Huber, Elfi's father, had chosen us was an incredible honor! He was the director of the club and had organized the event.

Let me gently take your hand
Help you understand
Let me hold you in my arms
Wipe your tears away.

Let me be your guiding light
Shining in the night
Trust in me to see you through,
Count on me. I love you.

Love heals everything
Love is all we need.

Love heals everything
Love is all there is.

(©Francine Jarry)

Chapter Fourteen

Our New "Family"

Mr. Huber came to get us at the cooking school the following day. We took a streetcar to his home. It was close to the Prater, Vienna's famous amusement park. The Riesenrad, the Prater's giant ferris wheel, could be seen from much of Vienna.

Elfi and her mother greeted us at the door with hugs. Both were smiling, as were we. Smiles and hand gestures were our main ways of communicating because we spoke different languages.

The Hubers' apartment was cosy and tastefully furnished. Elfi took us to her room and motioned for us to put down our bags. She and her mother had made up beds for us there. I glanced around the room, looking for the baby Jesus doll. I spotted it on Elfi's bed. I ran over, grabbed it, and hugged it tight. I was never going to let it go! Elfi smiled, as did her parents. She said the word *"Puppe,"* which means "doll." I repeated the word. This was the first of many German lessons I received at the Huber home.

"Are you hungry?" Mrs. Huber asked us. We nodded eagerly. We were always ready to eat! She gave us some delicious cauliflower soup and potato salad. After we finished eating, I saw some playing cards on a coffee table. I decided to show the Hubers how to play Gypsy Rummy, but Zsuzsi started protesting and yelling at me, as usual. She tried to tell the Hubers that I cheated. I didn't actually cheat. I was just a very imaginative player who constantly saw new possibilities and combinations in the cards. I put no limits on myself when I played, and I often changed the rules. This was *my* game, and the fact that no one understood *my* rules was *not* my problem!

The Hubers scratched their heads in confusion, as I proceeded to put down some creative card combinations. When they tried to put down similar hands, I shook my head and said "no" to their attempts at gaining points. My sister was screaming at me now, which made the Hubers even more curious.

Then, the unthinkable happened—Mr. Huber pretended he knew the game. He winked at Zsuzsi and said something to Elfi and her mother. They nodded in agreement. It was the beginning of my undoing. The Hubers started putting down ridiculous card combinations, and Zsuzsi gave them the go-ahead, as if she were now in charge of the game. I was outnumbered and outsuckered! Elfi ended up beating me with her made-up rules.

I had finally met my match! I pouted, of course, and Zsuzsi laughed uncontrollably. The Hubers laughed, too, and then Elfi started tickling me. Zsuzsi joined in and showed Elfi my most ticklish spots. Soon, I was squealing at the top of my lungs. The tickling then broke out into an all-out, three-way pillow fight.

We were soon all sweaty, so Mrs. Huber decided to give us a bath. The Hubers didn't have a built-in bathtub. They filled a big metal tub with warm water in the kitchen. Before we undressed, we pointed to the door and yelled at Mr. Huber in two languages, "No men allowed!" Mr. Huber pretended to cry about being left out of the bathtime fun. His wife smiled at him and closed the kitchen door. The three of us girls took baths, one after the other. Then Mrs. Huber gave us some clean pajamas to wear.

Clean and dressed, we came out to the living room to say goodnight to Mr. Huber. He pointed to his wife and then to himself and said, "Aunt Burgi, Uncle Hans." In that moment, we became family. I felt safe and very loved by these people that I'd just met.

The Huber Family: Uncle Hans, Aunt Burgi, and Elfi. This picture was taken around the time my sister and I lived with them.

Life with the Hubers was a lot of fun! They did everything they could to make us feel comfortable. Elfi was on Christmas holidays from school, so we were with her all day. She and Aunt Burgi taught us German words and phrases, and soon we could answer simple questions with simple answers. We liked speaking German and started to feel more and more like Austrians.

Elfi took us shopping each morning to buy the food that her mother would prepare that day. At that time, people shopped daily for the freshest milk, bread, fruits, and vegetables. But unlike in Hungary, the shoppers didn't have to line up for hours to buy their food. We bought bread at the bakery and fruits and vegetables at the grocery store. Elfi made us ask in German for the food we needed. We shopped and learned German at the same time. We loved going shopping because we met a lot of friendly people. Elfi introduced us as her new "sisters." We were so proud!

The food in Vienna amazed us—even the food in cans. Zsuzsi and I had never seen canned food before and couldn't help but wonder how people got the food out. We were also surprised to see so many fresh fruits and vegetables in winter. In Hungary, we preserved fruits and vegetables in special jars for the winter. Elfi got a kick out of our reactions. When we picked up some mandarin oranges and smelled them, she bought some for us as a treat. They smelled wonderful and were so easy to peel! Then we pointed to the bananas. She bought a few for us to eat later.

Most Austrians and Hungarians are Catholic. We were Catholic, and so were the Hubers. Catholics don't eat meat during

Advent, which is the four weeks before Christmas, so we didn't eat meat during our stay with the Hubers. We ate mainly vegetable soups with dumplings, as well as salads made from cabbage, beans, or cucumbers. We ate a lot of potatoes, too. Sometimes we had potato pancakes with sour cream. Zsuzsi, Elfi, and I helped Aunt Burgi cook these lunches and suppers. We were good at peeling potatoes, and we enjoyed cleaning the kitchen with Elfi.

Uncle Hans came home at around six o'clock each night with a different surprise. We couldn't wait for him to come home because he was so much fun! He reminded me of my grandfather. We never knew when he was serious or kidding. One night, he came in the door and said that he'd found something on the street he thought we might like. He said it was in the hall. We couldn't imagine what it could be. When we went to the door and looked out into the hallway, we saw our parents! The Hubers had invited them for dinner. That night, they told us that our parents would be spending Christmas with us. Nothing could have made us happier.

We loved Uncle Hans. He made us laugh.

Stille Nacht, heilige Nacht,

Alles schläft, einsam wacht

Nur das traute, hochheilige Paar,

Holder Knabe im lockigen Haar

Schlaf in himmlischer Ruh'!

Schlaf in himmlischer Ruh'!

Silent night, holy night,

All is calm, all is bright

Round yon Virgin Mother and Child,

Holy Infant so tender and mild

Sleep in heavenly peace!

Sleep in heavenly peace!

Chapter Fifteen

Christmas is Here at Last!

In most of Europe, Christmas is celebrated on Christmas Eve instead of on Christmas Day. In Hungary, the gifts are brought by the Christ Child, the Christmas Angel, and her helper angels. I wondered if the Christmas Angel would find us in Austria. We weren't that far from home, but we *were* in another world!

On the morning of December 24th, Uncle Hans asked Elfi to take us back to the cooking school, where our parents were waiting. He said we would be eating lunch there. I couldn't figure out why, but I trusted he knew. He also said, with the help of some sign language, "You'll come back later with Mommy and Daddy."

That made me happy! We would have Mom and Dad here with us on Christmas Eve, and Tamás would have his parents with him at his host family's home, as well. We put on our coats and made our way to the cooking school. When we arrived, we ran upstairs as quickly as we could. We couldn't wait to see our parents. We found everyone in the big room, where we slept when we lived at the cooking school.

All the children were there that day, even though most of them were staying in Austrian homes over Christmas. The nuns knew that we'd be with our Austrian families for the evening, so they wanted to celebrate Christmas with us during the day. The aroma of the wonderful food they had cooked for us filled the building.

While we waited for lunch to be ready, we found out what everyone had been doing over the past few days. Dad told us that he'd sold some of his blood to make a little money. Mom and Aunt Ica had volunteered to wash dishes at the cooking school. Mom had also written some letters and visited Aunt Rózsi a couple of times. There was still no news from my grandparents because the letters weren't getting through. I was happy to have this worrisome conversation interrupted by a cheerful nun who announced, "Lunch is served!"

We raced to the dining room and saw a huge buffet of fresh fruit, colorful vegetable dishes, steaming hot bean soup, freshly baked bread and rolls, a variety of cheeses, rolled pancakes with cottage-cheese filling, and my favorite small dumplings, called *Spätzle*, which were topped with mushrooms. For dessert, there were strudels, as well as the famous Austrian cake, *Sachertorte*. *Sachertorte* is a chocolate cake with jam under the icing. It was delicious! It reminded me of Hungarian cakes with jam fillings.

We loaded our plates and sat down to eat, after saying grace. Watching us enjoy our food made the nuns smile. They felt proud that their cooking students had made such an amazing feast! We praised their culinary skills with our huge appetites, joyful smiles,

and many compliments. Elfi made friends with a nun who was just a few years older than she was. She chatted happily with her new friend and helped clear the tables.

Just after we finished lunch, Aunt Rózsi and Uncle Karl appeared at the dining room door. They had a letter for us. We got up from the table and rushed over to hug them and wish them a Merry Christmas. Aunt Rózsi handed us the letter from our grandparents, which had a Vienna postmark. My grandfather had managed to find a man who was planning to escape and paid him to mail the letter to us when he arrived in Vienna.

In the letter, my grandmother said that many people in our town had been taken to jail. She now realized that we'd made the right decision to leave because the ÁVOs *did* come looking for my father. She then shared some news about our family. Aunt Joli had not heard from Uncle János, so she and her two daughters were now living with my grandparents. And, right after we left, Marika and Miklós moved into our apartment. We were relieved that our belongings had not fallen into the hands of strangers, but my father wasn't at all happy to hear that Uncle Miklós was riding his motorcycle. That motorcycle had been my father's pride and joy!

In her letter, Grandmama told Zsuzsi and me to visit all the beautiful castles in Vienna for her, especially Schönbrunn Castle, where her favorite queen, Queen Elisabeth of Hungary, once lived. She added that she'd be with us in spirit on Christmas Eve and made us promise to be happy. As Zsuzsi and I nodded in agreement, tears rolled down our cheeks. We missed our grandparents a lot!

We thanked Aunt Rózsi and Uncle Karl for visiting us and for bringing the letter. It connected us with our family in Hungary on this very special day. We gave the nuns big hugs and thanked them again for the wonderful feast. We wished them a Merry Christmas. I wondered if they would be with *their* families on Christmas Eve.

We left the cooking school and went back to the Hubers' apartment. When we arrived, it was almost dark. Uncle Hans told us that we'd be going to a Christmas candlelight mass at seven o'clock. We barely got in the door, and it was time to leave again.

We arrived at the church early and listened to the choir sing beautiful Christmas carols. The music took me back to our Christmases in Hungary. Christmas there was such a magical time! I wondered if I would ever experience it in the same way again.

On December 24th each year, Zsuzsi and I were taken on an outing by one of our aunts. We went on long walks, or to the movies, or to visit friends, and we didn't come home until it was almost dark.

When we returned, our parents told us to wait in the kitchen until we heard the tinkling of "angel bells." If we entered the living room before we heard the bells, we would risk scaring away the angels. Finally, the bells signaled that we could go in.

As we entered the dark room, we noticed the Christmas tree right away. It was covered in angel hair and illuminated by real candles and sparklers. The tree and decorations told us that the Christmas Angel and Christ Child had already been there. There were also some unwrapped gifts under the tree.

The gifts were not big. Sometimes we received clothes or small toys. The tree, with all the sweets it contained, was considered to be the main gift. It was loaded with cookies, as well as candies wrapped in tissue paper and shiny foil. These special Christmas candies were called *"szalon cukor."*

Before our parents allowed us to look at the presents, we had to sing a Christmas carol called *"Mennyböl az Angyal."*

We sang these words in Hungarian:

Mennyböl az angyal, lejött hozzátok,
pásztorok, pásztorok!
Hogy Betlehembe sietve menvén,
lássátok, lássátok.

In English, the carol is called "Angel from Heaven." Sometimes we sang other carols as well, such as "Silent Night," but we always started with this one. For Zsuzsi and me, it was pure torture to have to sing, when all we wanted to do was look at our presents and take some treats off the tree.

We thought the angels made the cookies that were hanging on the tree, but I later found out that they had been made by my mother, grandmother, and aunts. The cookies were baked in the shapes of bells, pretzels, crescent moons, stars, Christmas trees, and circles with scalloped edges. We were allowed to eat something off the tree every day until January 6th, the twelfth and last day of Christmas, when the tree was taken down. By then, it was usually bare.

After receiving our presents, we had a meal of vegetable or fish soup and plum dumplings coated with sugar and breadcrumbs. We talked, sang, played with our gifts, and listened to Christmas stories told by my grandparents.

We then went to Midnight Mass. After church, Grandmama brought out everyone's favorite Christmas food—*kocsonya*, which is pickled pigs' feet in aspic. Aspic is broth that turns to jelly when it gets cold. Actually, it wasn't everyone's favorite food. Zsuzsi and I found it totally disgusting! It was our traditional Christmas Eve meal, but Zsuzsi and I preferred to snack on slices of *kalács* instead. *Kalács* was a rolled cake filled with walnuts or poppyseeds. Most Hungarians call this cake *beigli*, but our family called it *kalács*.

We had no idea what would happen on Christmas Eve in Vienna, but we were about to find out! We knew that Austrian children believed in *Christkindl*, but we didn't know about their traditions. *Christkindl*, which means "Christ Child," was like our Christmas Angel and Baby Jesus rolled into one.

When we came home from church, Aunt Burgi warmed up the huge meal that she'd cooked earlier that day. We were very hungry. It was about nine o'clock by then, which was a long time since lunch! There were several kinds of salads, a potato casserole, and fried fish called carp. The meal was delicious, and we loved every bite! My parents especially enjoyed the fish.

After our meal, Uncle Hans went into the living room and closed the door behind him. This really made us wonder what was up! Before long, however, we heard the tinkling of tiny bells. Uncle Hans came out and said he'd heard *Christkindl* leave, so we could now go into the living room.

The room was dark, but we could see a sparkling Christmas tree inside. It had flickering electric candles on it, which looked just like real candles. As we came closer, we all joined hands, and my mother started singing "Angel from Heaven." Uncle Hans, Aunt Burgi, and Elfi hummed along. I could see their lovely faces in the darkness, and I wished my grandparents could be with us.

After singing our Hungarian carol, we sang "Silent Night" in German. I admired the tree as we sang. Hanging from its branches were colorful glass bulbs and ornaments in the shapes of animals and angels. Tucked into the tree were chocolate coins wrapped in gold foil, as well as cookies and candies. Under the tree were presents wrapped in shiny paper. Was there one for me?

Uncle Hans handed a gift to Aunt Burgi. When she opened it, she found a colorful silk scarf. She loved it and put it around her neck. My mother received a blue blouse with gold buttons. She ran right into our room to put it on. We all agreed that she looked beautiful in it. My father's present was a pair of leather gloves, which he needed badly. His old gloves were torn and dirty. Elfi received a sweater and skirt. The outfit was very stylish, and I couldn't wait to see it on her. Uncle Hans's gift was a leather wallet, and Zsuzsi got a stuffed toy dog, which she named Oskar. She hugged it and talked to it non-stop. I was the only one who hadn't received a gift.

Uncle Hans finally picked up the last package, which he handed to me. I opened it to find a baby doll that was just like Elfi's doll. I burst into tears and hugged the Hubers and my parents. That night, I fell asleep with my new doll and had no nightmares.

When Elfi, Zsuzsi, and I woke early the next morning, the apartment was still very quiet. We tiptoed into the kitchen and noticed a huge pile of dirty dishes. We motioned to one another that we would clean up and make breakfast for our parents. We made a game of washing the dishes as quietly as we could. Elfi washed, and we dried. We worked quickly and silently, and soon the kitchen sparkled. Then we started breakfast. We boiled some eggs, cut them in half, and added some slices of ham, cheese, and bread to make a beautiful breakfast platter. When the food was ready, we put on the coffee. The smell of coffee woke our parents.

Aunt Burgi and Mom were very happy to see the clean kitchen. They hugged us and wished us a Merry Christmas. Dad and Uncle Hans also came into the kitchen. Everyone enjoyed the meal we had made. After a few minutes, there was nothing left!

Uncle Hans told us to look out the window. It had snowed all night, and Vienna was covered in a fluffy white blanket! He suggested we bundle up and go for a walk, but Aunt Burgi had a better idea—a sleigh ride in Old Vienna. We thought that sounded wonderful, so we dressed quickly and headed to the center of town. It wasn't long before we found a horse-drawn sleigh. We climbed in and covered ourselves in heavy fur blankets. As we rode through the park, the bells on our sleigh sounded just like the bells of the Christmas Angel. On hearing the bells, people waved to us and shouted in German, *"Fröhliche Weihnachten!"* We shouted back in Hungarian, *"Kellemes Karácsonyi ünnepeket!"* Both meant "Merry Christmas." It was a very merry Christmas indeed!

How do you say goodbye?

When I became a refugee,

"goodbye" was the word I said most often.

I said my goodbyes to my family

and friends in Hungary.

That was heartbreaking.

Now I had to say goodbye to another family

whom I loved and who loved me.

I said goodbye again,

but I carried the Hubers with me

in my heart.

I never stopped loving them.

Chapter Sixteen

The Last Days with the Hubers

The last day of the year was fast approaching. Soon, it would be time for Elfi to start school again and for us to return to the cooking school. We'd been with the Hubers for almost three weeks now. During these three weeks, Tamás had been living with another Austrian family, who had a daughter named Zuliani. Zuliani and Elfi were friends, so we saw Tamás almost every day.

Several times during our stay with the Hubers, my sister left the apartment without telling anyone where she was going. Each time she left, she went to see Tamás, but she always came home in time for lunch.

So, when Zsuzsi took off one day, we just thought she was at Zuliani's. She *did* go to Zuliani's, but then she left again with Tamás. She and Tamás told Zuliani that they were going to the Hubers' apartment. When Zsuzsi wasn't home at lunchtime, Aunt Burgi told Elfi and me to go get her. We went to Zuliani's, only to be told that my sister and Tamás were supposed to be with us. This time, both Zsuzsi and Tamás had run away!

We were all in a state of panic! Where could they be? We ran from shop to shop in Kaisermühlen, where the Hubers lived. We asked people if anyone had seen the kids, but no one had. Finally, a customer at the bakery overheard us and said she'd seen two kids walking toward the Prater, and one of them was pointing to the ferris wheel.

Zsuzsi and Tamás had hatched a plot to go to the Prater. The Prater was closed for the winter, but they'd noticed that the Riesenrad, the huge ferris wheel, was turning during Christmas week. They decided to go on the ride without letting us know about their plans.

We knew instantly that the children the woman had described must be Tamás and Zsuzsi! Elfi, Zuliani, and I hopped on a streetcar. We promised Aunt Burgi that we would bring the runaways back home. We were soon at the Prater. We walked around and saw people trying to win prizes at the ball-toss booths and shooting galleries, but there was no sign of Tamás or Zsuzsi.

We were starving, so we bought some wieners for lunch. Elfi asked the woman who sold the wieners if she'd seen two kids who were by themselves. She said that a Hungarian boy and girl were there not half an hour ago, looking longingly at her food, so she gave them a wiener each, as well as an orange soda. She said the children were heading toward the Riesenrad.

We ate quickly and also took off for the ferris wheel. We arrived just in time to see Tamás and Zsuzsi get on. Instead of open seats, the ferris wheel had large cars that could hold several people.

Tamás and Zsuzsi were already inside one of the cars. We ran over to the ticket booth and told the attendant our problem.

"Are those the kids?" he asked pointing to the car, already knowing the answer. "I don't think you'll get them to come out, so why don't you all go on the ride for free?"

We were angry and delighted at the same time. When we climbed into the car, I blasted Tamás and Zsuzsi for running away, but they didn't seem the least bit sorry!

"We saw the ferris wheel turning, and we wanted to go on it," my sister said. "We were bored. You and Elfi always have fun together, but I feel left out." Then Tamás piped in, "And I like Zuliani, but she's much older than me. Zsuzsi and I just wanted to have some fun. What's wrong with that?"

"I'll tell you what's wrong," I shouted, sounding a lot like my mother, "you had us all worried to death!"

I don't think I got through to them. They were having too much fun. When the Riesenrad started moving, the cars rocked in the wind as they climbed upward. Zsuzsi and Tamás loved the rocking, but the motion made me feel sick, so I took a deep breath and stopped talking. As we reached the top of the wheel, the scene took my breath away! I could see most of Vienna from there, and it was a wonderful view! The sun made the city glow as if all its buildings were covered in gold.

The ride took only a few minutes, but it seemed like hours to me. I had the sensation that I was seeing everything in slow motion. I was in another space, another time, another universe.

The Riesenrad is over 200 feet (61 m) tall. The view at the top was spectacular!

When the ride was over, we got off and took the streetcar home to Elfi's apartment. We guessed Zuliani's mother would be there as well. Both Aunt Burgi and Zuliani's mother were happy to see Zsuzsi and Tamás and weren't angry. They did, however, insist that the two kids never leave home again unless Elfi or Zuliani was with them. When Uncle Hans came home that night and heard what had happened, he laughed and said he should take our picture in case any of us went missing again!

From left to right; Zsuzsi, Zuliani, Tamás, me, and Elfi. This picture was taken after Tamás and Zsuzsi's "great escape" to the Prater.

The last day we spent with the Hubers was the last day of 1956. It was New Year's Eve, and there was a huge party at the Kaisermühlen sports club, where we had attended the Christmas party three weeks earlier. After the party, all the children who had been staying with Austrian families would go back with their parents. Zsuzsi and Tamás didn't seem to mind, but I felt terribly sad. I'd become very attached to the Hubers.

Uncle Hans and the other organizers of the party worked hard to make the evening fun, but many people were crying. The Hungarian guests were remembering the events of 1956, and I was crying because I had to leave Elfi and her parents that night. Leaving the Hubers was like losing everyone I loved all over again—especially Elfi, my new best friend.

I wished I could take Elfi with me. I loved having her as an older sister, and she said she'd always longed for younger sisters. Elfi was quiet, intelligent, and sensitive. She and I were both thinkers and dreamers. If only I could have known Elfi's thoughts and dreams! This was the only part of the friendship that was missing—we couldn't share our thoughts or communicate our dreams because we spoke different languages.

I would miss Aunt Burgi, too. She was always cheerful and enthusiastic. She was the person I needed then to help me trust and feel safe again. She gave me a strong hand to hold when my mother's hand was shaky. She looked at me with love, and I felt loveable. She hugged me when I needed to be held. I am forever grateful for her love.

Uncle Hans was the most wonderful man I'd ever met! He called himself our *"Huberpapschi,"* which means "Huber Daddy." We couldn't wait for Uncle Hans to come home after work. The apartment was immediately filled with laughter. He played tricks on us, chased us around, tickled us, and made faces when we were too serious. He made us feel like we were his daughters.

Midnight came, and we heard church bells ringing in the new year, 1957. On hearing the bells, we sang both the Hungarian and Austrian anthems. There wasn't a dry eye in the house. It was then time to say goodbye. I hugged the Hubers.

"Thank you," I managed to say between sobs to Aunt Burgi, Uncle Hans, and Elfi. "I love you, and I'll never forget you."

I cried all the way back to the cooking school. My mother practically had to carry me up the stairs. I was very weak, but I found my old air mattress and tried to get some sleep. Not a chance! I started throwing up almost as soon as my head hit the pillow. I threw up all night long. Everything that I had pushed down, all the loss and sadness of 1956, was coming up at once.

Finally, there was nothing left to throw up. My mother gave me a bath before putting me to bed. I was shaking, and so was my mother. We'd both been up the whole night. It was nearly dawn.

Mom dressed me in clean pajamas. We both fell onto our mattresses, hoping that our ordeal was over. I fell asleep for a short time and then woke up screaming from my now-familiar nightmare. I hugged the doll that the *Christkindl* had brought me for Christmas. Eventually, I fell asleep again.

Are you missing

if you don't know someone is looking for you?

Are you lost

if you know where you are?

Do you ever

just not want to be found?

Vienna was a great place to hide.

It was a fantasy city

made for daydreaming and pretending.

Zsuzsi, Tamás, and Éva

went missing in Vienna,

and I found myself there.

Chapter Seventeen
Eva is Missing!

Most of the people at the cooking school went to church on New Year's Day, so my mother and I were able to get some sleep when they left. We woke up at lunchtime, just when my father arrived. Celia was with him.

During our last week with the Hubers, a lot had happened in my parents' world about which I knew nothing. With Celia's help, my father had obtained four visas to the United States. They were worth their weight in gold! The United States was not admitting very many refugees, and most people wanted to go there. Even though other countries offered to accept Hungarians, many people were staying in Austria in the hopes of getting American visas.

My mother's sisters lived in Canada, so my mother wanted us to move there. Her sisters had sponsored us, and our visas were already in the works. I had always assumed that we'd be living with, or near, my aunts and cousins, so imagine how shocked I was to learn that my father had other plans in mind for us. He'd made up his mind to live in the United States, and Celia supported him all the way. My father had always wanted to live in the States, and, in the beginning, he stood his ground. But *we* wanted to be with our relatives! Tamás's parents weren't able to get visas for the United States, but they *did* receive visas for Canada. Since my parents and Tamás's parents were best friends, my father agreed that our families should live near one another. He finally gave in. We would all go to Canada. He should have known this from the start. With three females in the family, he seldom got his way.

Still, my father held on to our American visas until he was certain we were on our way to Canada. Only at the last possible second did he reluctantly give them to some Hungarian friends, who couldn't believe their good fortune!

We were booked on the RMS Saxonia ocean liner and would be leaving Vienna to sail to Canada in about ten days. Tamás and his parents were also booked on that ship. This was great news! I didn't want to stay in Vienna any longer if I couldn't be with the Hubers, and I was starting to worry about missing school. By the time we were scheduled to arrive in Canada, I'd have missed more than three months of school, and I still had to learn English! I asked Celia if English was difficult to learn. She spoke English, as well as Hungarian, German, and French. She said she had a quick way of knowing whether or not I'd learn the language easily.

"Say 'butter'," she challenged me.

"Bootter," I answered, pronouncing it the German way.

"Try again," she said.

"Bahttrr." I tried to make the sound by rolling my tongue.

"Babi, until you can pronounce this word properly, you'll never speak English without an accent."

I was furious with Celia! How dare she insult me this way? From that point onward, I practiced saying "butter" a hundred times a day. The word became the symbol of the challenge I gave myself. I would learn to speak English so perfectly and so quickly that no one would ever know I wasn't born speaking it. And I did! To this day, I have the urge to find Celia and shout at her. "Butter! Butter!" But I suspect Celia knew what she was doing. She'd figured out by then that making me mad also made me want to prove her wrong.

It was a good thing that Aunt Rózsi and Uncle Karl showed up when they did. My mood changed immediately. My aunt and uncle came to wish us a Happy New Year and to bring us another letter. This one was from my Aunt Manci in Canada. She wrote that Blanka had arrived safely, and that the paperwork had been sent through for *our* visas, but no one knew where Éva was! In her letter, Aunt Manci asked if Éva was in Vienna with us.

"What? She's in Canada with you, of course!" my mother shouted, as if my aunt in Canada could hear her.

Then she turned to Aunt Rózsi. "Didn't you tell me that Éva had left Vienna?" She was shouting, as if it was Aunt Rózsi who'd done something wrong.

"I assumed Éva and her friend were already in Canada," Rózsi said, "because after they stayed at my apartment, I never heard from them again. I thought they had left Vienna long ago."

My mother was tired and irritable. After all, she'd been up half the night nursing me. I didn't know how she'd handle this. It was, as she put it, a catastrophe! Clearly, my mother imagined the worst.

My mother told us that she would not set foot on any ship until Éva was found. Luckily, Tamás's parents and Celia offered to help. Celia suggested that the adults visit the various immigration offices and ask whether they had any record of Éva. Surely, they'd be able to track her down! It was a good plan, but it meant leaving us kids alone all day at the cooking school.

"No problem," said Uncle Karl. "I'll take the three kids sightseeing when I'm not working during the day." Uncle Karl was a policeman who worked different shifts, so he often had his days free. Aunt Rózsi said he loved children, so he was looking forward to spending time with us.

While we were playing tourist in Vienna, my parents searched for Éva. At one of the immigration offices they visited, someone told my father that Éva's name was on a passenger list for a ship called the MS Berlin. Éva was scheduled to depart on this ship in the third week of January. She would be sailing from Bremerhaven, Germany. My father, with the help of Celia, explained that we were leaving on the RMS Saxonia in less than ten days. He asked if the immigration officer could transfer Éva to our ship. The man said he'd see what he could do. What my father didn't tell him, of course, was that Éva was missing!

My parents, Tamás's parents, and Celia combed the city looking for Éva at various refugee shelters. After a few days of searching, my father found Éva and her friend at a youth hostel, where she was having a good time with other young people. Éva had no idea we'd left Hungary or were in Vienna, just as we didn't know that she was *still* in Vienna.

As soon as my father found Éva, he went back to the immigration office to see if the officer had put her on our ship. It was almost time for us to leave Vienna. The man at the office informed my father that we were no longer leaving on the RMS Saxonia. We'd been transferred to the MS Berlin to be with Éva. My father was not at all happy about this change. We now had to stay longer in Vienna, and he wanted us to start our new lives as soon as possible. He argued with the man at the office, but our tickets had already been given away.

Fairy tales do come true,

when you let them happen to you.

Visiting Schönbrunn Palace

was like being part of a fairy tale.

Chapter Eighteen

Living the Fairy Tale

While everyone was searching for Aunt Éva, Uncle Karl became our babysitter and tour guide. Each day, he took us to different tourist attractions. I begged him to take us to Schönbrunn Palace! I'd heard that it was the most beautiful palace in the world. Uncle Karl promised he would take us there the very next day. He actually took us there three times in total! On our first trip to Schönbrunn, Aunt Rózsi came along. We were happy to have her there so we could ask her questions in Hungarian.

During the streetcar ride to the palace, Aunt Rózsi told us that Schönbrunn had been the home of the Habsburg royal family. The story of this family was closely linked with the history of Hungary.

A long time ago, Hungary was part of the Austrian Empire. This huge empire was governed by the Habsburg kings, who were called emperors. In 1848, the Hungarian people revolted against the Austrian government. That same year, a new Austrian emperor was crowned. His name was Franz Josef, and he was one of the Habsburgs who had lived at Schönbrunn Palace. As emperor, Franz Josef crushed the Hungarian Revolution with the help of the

Russian army—just as our Revolution had been crushed by Russian troops. But, in 1867, he agreed to a compromise, which gave Hungary its own government. The two countries became known as the Dual Monarchy of Austria-Hungary. Franz Josef and his wife Elisabeth, known as Queen Sisi, were crowned the king and queen of Hungary.

The people of Hungary fell in love with Queen Sisi because *she* loved them. She spent more time in Hungary than she did in Austria and learned to speak Hungarian fluently. In fact, Sisi's fourth and favorite child was born in Hungary. She was known as the "Hungarian child" because of her birthplace and because she spoke fluent Hungarian, just as her mother did. Her name was Marie Valerie, which is also my legal name.

One day, while I was still living in Hungary, I found some pictures hidden at my grandmother's house. They were pictures of Queen Sisi. Sisi was so beautiful that I wanted badly to show her pictures to my friends. But my grandmother was horrified when I asked her if I could borrow the pictures. She made me watch as she burned the pictures and told me never, ever to talk about them— or the queen. The Communists didn't want us remembering Hungary's past, so my grandmother was terrified that she would get into trouble for having such pictures at her home.

When Grandmama calmed down, she told me all about Queen Sisi because she knew how much I loved fairy tales. I had no idea then that I would ever be visiting Queen Sisi's home in Vienna. In her Christmas letter, Grandmama asked me to visit Schönbrunn for her, and here I was. I felt as if Grandmama was with me.

Queen Sisi was stunning! I wanted to show her pictures to my friends.

There was a lot more to learn about the Queen, but we were now at Schönbrunn and had to get off the streetcar. We were amazed when we saw the castle for the first time. Both the buildings and the gardens were magnificent—there were fountains everywhere! Uncle Karl took us to the entrance and got us passes. Unfortunately, he had to work that day, so he left us with Aunt Rózsi and went on his rounds in the city near the castle.

The tour we were taking allowed us to see about 40 of the palace's 1,440 rooms. As we walked through room after room, we were in awe of the beauty of this castle. There were ballrooms with pictures painted on the walls and ceilings. In my mind's eye, I could see men and women, dressed in beautiful clothes, dancing to the music of Mozart, a famous Austrian composer.

We finally reached Sisi's apartment. It was close to the garden, so the queen could go outdoors for walks or ride her horses without being noticed. Aunt Rózsi said that Sisi exercised many hours a day to stay slim. On her portraits, I noticed her beautiful long hair. Aunt Rózsi said it took several hours each day to brush and style it and a whole day to wash and dry it!

We reluctantly left Queen Sisi's apartment and continued the tour. Of all the rooms in the palace, the Mirrors Room surprised me the most. The mirrors on the walls of this room faced one another. When you looked into one mirror, it reflected another, which changed the appearance of the room completely. I felt like I was in another dimension. I wondered if what I saw was real! In one mirror, I thought I saw the reflection of Sisi. When I looked again, she was gone. Was I seeing her ghost?

The Millions Room took my breath away! It looked as if the whole room was covered in gold. In it were small panels of different sizes and shapes. Actual paintings were set into these panels. Apparently, members of the royal family had put these miniature paintings together to make a collage. The Millions Room was the most beautiful work of art I'd ever seen. In fact, the entire palace looked like a work of art! Never before or since have I seen a castle that even comes close to the beauty of Schönbrunn. I was sorry to leave it, but I knew I'd be back soon.

For the next two weeks, Uncle Karl took us out sightseeing almost every day. We visited the Schönbrunn Zoo and toured the Parliament Buildings and the Austrian National Library. We watched horses perform difficult routines and jumps at the Winter Riding School. We also visited Belvedere Castle.

Belvedere Castle contained wonderful works of art, but the whole of Schönbrunn Palace was a work of art!

One day, we even climbed the South Tower of St. Stephen's Cathedral, Vienna's most famous church. This tower, called *Steffl*, was 445 feet (136 m) high. As we climbed, we counted the steps out loud in German. It took us 343 steps to reach the top! We wheezed out the last number—*drei hundert und drei und vierzig*! After the final step, we entered a small room with windows. The view was magnificent and definitely worth the climb! We could see almost all of Vienna from there.

Soon after Éva was found, Tamás and his family left Vienna. My parents, sister, Éva, and I spent our last days in Vienna, seeing everything we could possibly see. We even visited Schönbrunn together. This was my fourth visit. I knew so much about it by then that I could have written a book! I didn't hesitate to show off my knowledge to my parents and aunt about the Dual Monarchy and about Queen Sisi, who had once been our Queen, too.

"I think the girl is ready to go back to school!" Éva said. "By the way Babi, how is your English?"

"Butter and butter," I replied in English, but she didn't get my joke. "Say 'butter', Éva." I said, giggling.

"Bootter," Éva said. "Isn't that a German word?"

"Yes, but it's also English, and in English it's pronounced very differently. If you can't get it right, you'll never speak the English language without an accent."

"How did I do?" she asked.

"Not well!" I teased.

Éva smacked my bottom, and we both laughed out loud. I'd missed Éva since she left Hungary. It was fun to be with her again.

(above) We could see most of Vienna from the South Tower.
(top right) We went to the Austrian National Library, the oldest library in the world. I've always loved books and libraries.
(right) We watched horses perform jumps and routines at the Winter Riding School.

There's always another boat,

another chance, a new beginning.

Always another boat,

another door, waiting to open.

Always another boat,

another dream unfolding.

Anytime you begin,

you begin to let it in,

all that you've been wanting

will come flowing.

(© Francine Jarry)

Chapter Nineteen
On Our Way "Home"

The day had finally arrived. We were leaving our beloved Vienna, which felt like home to us now. My mother kept trying to pack our belongings. She looked at all the things we'd received in Austria and shook her head. It was amazing how much "stuff" we'd accumulated in such a short time. We couldn't possibly take it all with us! We sorted through our clothes and toys and tried to figure out what we would need in Canada. We left the rest for the new refugees at the cooking school.

Most of the people I knew at the cooking school were now gone, but other refugees had replaced those who'd left. I didn't make friends with them because I knew I was leaving soon, too. I missed Elfi a lot, and memories of my life in Hungary also made me feel sad these days. I missed Zsuzsa, and there was a great big hole in my life that used to be filled by my grandparents. I even missed school. I wondered who would get the top marks in fourth grade and win the prize now that I was gone. Would it be Margit? Would she enjoy winning without me as her competitor?

I wondered about the future, and I was very afraid. One of the few things that made me feel better was knowing we had family waiting for us. I hoped my cousins would like me. What if they didn't want to be friends because I couldn't speak English?

I was quiet as we packed, and so was my mother. I knew she had similar thoughts. It must have been scary for her and my father to start brand new lives, especially at their ages. I hoped they were comforted by the fact that we would have my aunts and Tamás's family with us. I know I was.

The nuns told us to be ready to leave the cooking school in an hour. Buses would be picking us up, along with the other refugees who were on their way out of Vienna. The buses would take us to the train station. There, we would board trains bound for Bremerhaven, in the northern part of Germany.

With packed bags in hand, we looked around the cooking school. We were leaving another home we'd grown to love. We would miss the fun and the wonderful meals made by the students! The nuns hugged us goodbye, and we thanked them. How absolutely fabulous they'd been to us!

I wept as we drove through Vienna. The city had quickly become my city. I knew it well and loved it. It felt like home to me now. Even at my age, I understood what the people of Vienna had given me. They'd given me the gift of gratitude. In Vienna, there was always something for which to give thanks. I believed there were angels everywhere, and their main job was to show us how happy we could be.

We felt very sad to leave Vienna. Zsuzsi and I couldn't smile for the picture. This is the bus that took us to the train. Left to right in the back row are my mother, Éva, my dad, and Éva's friend, whose name was also Éva.

Our bus stopped at different shelters, picking up refugees. Other buses picked up refugees, as well. In no time, hundreds of us were getting off buses and preparing to board trains. As we lined up on the platform, another unexpected thing happened—a group of people appeared, bearing gifts such as chocolate bars, orange soda, fresh fruit, and various other treats! The generosity of the Austrians amazed us—right to the end of our stay.

Our family boarded the train and found seats. We tried to make ourselves as comfortable as possible for the long journey ahead. The books and magazines we'd brought along helped pass the

time, but when Zsuzsi and I grew restless, we walked the length of the train and talked to the other Hungarian children on board. As the train chugged along, we made many friends.

The train stopped often, and, at almost every station, people were gathered outside to greet us. The greetings and gifts continued throughout Austria, as well as Germany—all the way to Bremerhaven. People were showing their support for us "freedom fighters" and cheered us on for our courage.

After an eternity on the train, we arrived at a camp, where we'd be staying for three or four days. Each cabin at the camp had about ten cots, so we were again sharing a room with strangers. We went to a large hall for our meals. For the first time in weeks, we ate ordinary food that wasn't delicious.

This map shows our route so far, from Magyaróvár to Bremerhaven. In 1957, Germany was two countries: West Germany and East Germany.

People at the camp told horror stories about the voyage ahead. They'd heard that some of the ships that carried refugees across the ocean were war ships with great big cabins shared by several hundred passengers. The passengers slept in hammocks and were served slop for food. We envisioned big pots of porridge being doled out by scary men. We thought they would definitely be using huge wooden paddles, and we convinced ourselves that they would beat us kids with the paddles if we were bad. We named the Berlin "the floating prison."

The day soon came to board the ship. We packed our bags again and walked the "plank" up to the Berlin. It wasn't really a plank—it was a gangway—but we were playing pirates with the friends we'd made at the camp.

Together, we waited in line at the top of the gangway. How clean the ship seemed. It was actually sparkling! Armed with our grizzly expectations, we had no idea what we'd find once we boarded. After our names were checked off, we entered the ship and followed a steward to our cabin.

Our cabin was small, with two sets of bunk beds, but it had a closet for our clothes and a bathroom with a shower. The steward told us to be in the dining room in an hour. The captain would welcome us there and then hold a safety drill. After putting away our bags, we told our parents that we'd meet them in the dining room. We then ran upstairs quickly to have a look around the ship. You wouldn't believe what we saw! It was beyond our wildest dreams to be on a ship like this.

Beauty and comfort surrounded us. The MS Berlin was a spectacular ocean liner! We learned that it was built in Sweden and was known as the Gripsholm, until it was sold to a German company, Norddeutscher Lloyd, in 1954. It was then repainted and refurbished. The Berlin had the largest swimming pool of any ship—not that we could swim in January.

Obviously, this ship was not the floating prison we'd imagined it to be. In fact, the Berlin was quite the opposite! The ship was nicknamed the "floating palace." It had a luxurious dining room and tastefully decorated salons. I especially liked the card room, where tables were set up solely for the purpose of playing cards. We played many card games on the ship, including a new one I mastered, called Canasta. I learned it quickly and was soon challenging children and adults to try to beat me.

Meals on the Berlin were exquisite culinary adventures. We'd never seen food like this before! Although the cooking school in Vienna had served delicious meals, I knew nothing of the international cuisine that was prepared on this ship. The food was anything but the slop we'd imagined. The variety and the quality of the meals on the Berlin simply amazed us!

This 1957 menu shows the wonderful food served on the Berlin.

The buffet contained many kinds of fruits and cheeses, and we also had a daily menu with several choices. There was a children's menu, as well, but I definitely preferred the adult food. And I loved being served by stewards, who brought us whatever we asked for!

One day as I sat down for dinner, I noticed that our table's legs were secured to the floor, and the edges of the tabletop flipped up. This puzzled me. I flipped up the table's edges and asked the steward, "Why?" He immediately started walking as if he were drunk and indicated big waves on the ocean. I shrugged my shoulders and wondered what the heck he was talking about. For the past few days, the ocean had been calm and nothing inside the ship had moved. Still, the steward flashed me a knowing smile. He knew I would soon understand what he meant!

The following day, big ocean waves made being on the ship feel like a roller-coaster ride. Not only did the Berlin go up and down on the waves, it also rocked from side to side. It wasn't long before most of the passengers were throwing up. My parents and Éva were very ill and hardly left the cabin. Zsuzsi and I were also throwing up, but somehow we willed ourselves to get better. I'm sure the other kids did the same, so they wouldn't miss all the fun.

There were many kids on the ship, and our parents let us run free and stay out as late as we wished. Most of the adults were too seasick to care what we kids were doing. They had no idea that we were having the time of our lives! We played cards, listened to the band, learned to dance the cha-cha, and met for afternoon tea.

I didn't count how many days we were at sea. The bad weather lengthened our journey, however. That much I knew. After seeing nothing but water for more than a week, we finally spotted land. I was a bit sad to have our fun voyage come to an end. Zsuzsi and I had made some really good friends, and very few of them were going to Canada. We had to say goodbye, yet again, to people we'd grown to love.

The Statue of Liberty and huge skyscrapers confirmed it—we were coming into New York. It was a famous city, a wondrous city, and at last we would see it—even if it was just from the ship. My father, who stood next to me on deck, sighed so loudly I could hear him. He desperately wanted to stay! I let out a sigh, as well.

All I could think of was how hard it was to lose my newest friends. Many people were leaving us now. Some were starting new lives in the United States, and others were changing ships and sailing on to South American countries, such as Brazil.

Our journey also was not yet over. We would stay on the Berlin and sail from New York to Nova Scotia, Canada, and from there, we would take a train to *our* new home.

When I finally walked down the gangway of the MS Berlin at Pier 21 in Halifax on February 6, 1957, I was no longer Kálmán Babi, refugee child. Being a refugee child was one of the greatest adventures of my life! But now, I was ready for the next big adventure—my life as Bobbie Kalman, immigrant.

And that life was about to begin…

From Refugee Child to Children's Author

From Refugee to Author

Some people might say that I'm an "immigrant success story." I've been an author and publisher for 30 years, and I'm well known for my books, but the first ten years of my life as an immigrant were anything but easy!

When we arrived in Canada, nothing happened the way we expected. We had planned to live in Ottawa, where my aunts Manci and Blanka, as well as Tamás's family, were living. Instead, we ended up in the suburbs of Toronto where, I'm sure, we were the only immigrants! We were supposed to live with my Aunt Ditti and her family, but they moved to another town shortly after we arrived. Suddenly, we were alone, without a support system. And the suburbs where we lived were cold, bleak, and really ugly! The colors in my life were gone again. I wanted to go back to Vienna or even to Communist Hungary.

When my sister and I started school, we were both put into the first grade, and the teacher asked us to sit at the very back of the class because she didn't know what to do with us. For almost a month, we were the invisible children in the class. If we put up our hands to answer a question, the teacher looked the other way.

Fortunately, two other teachers rescued my sister and me. They took us out of the first grade and placed us in the grades where we belonged. In fourth grade, I learned English in record time, and without an accent. I then skipped two grades, was at the top of my class, and graduated from elementary school when I was twelve. Years later, when I was a high-school student-teacher, I taught English to one of the students from my fourth-grade class!

(right) I studied hard, learned English quickly—and without an accent—and skipped two grades.

(below) My family was finally safe, but we didn't feel welcome.

We were happy to have our first car so we could drive to Toronto, where there were other Hungarians.

I loved studying, but I hated school. Although I looked like everyone else and spoke perfect English, I didn't fit in because I was an immigrant. I couldn't wait for Sundays to come. We went to a Hungarian church in Toronto, where we could be with other families from our culture. We made many friends there. I couldn't be Hungarian in Hungary, but I never thought Canada was the place where I'd become a true Hungarian! I learned to dance the *csárdás*, the Hungarian national dance, and became a debutante. I now realize that I wouldn't have had these wonderful experiences if I'd been accepted by my suburban classmates.

Manci   Ditti

My grandparents visited us in 1963. It was the first time in 25 years that they saw their two oldest daughters!

When I was 15, we moved next door to a Ukrainian family, who became our best friends. I am forever grateful for their love and support. Here, their daughter Tina and I are dressed for a Roman banquet at my school. Her mother Jeanette made our costumes.

(left) My sister and cousins helped celebrate my birthday. I'm the one wearing the dress with the bow. The two cousins on my left and right looked a lot like me!

(right) Christmases were always big celebrations at our house. My mother still decorated our tree with **szalon cukor**.

At 19, I still lived in a Hungarian world. I became a debutante with the Hungarian Helicon Society in 1967. I'm in the center, behind the queen.

I graduated from university with degrees in English, Psychology, and Education. I was certified to teach both high school and elementary school. My first job as a teacher was at a special education school in Nassau, Bahamas.

My life changed when I moved to Nassau. The beauty and the colors of the island took my breath away! I loved my job, and I found a fabulous house to rent with three other teachers. To be able to live and work in such a different world was like a dream. There, I was bitten by the travel bug. I wanted to see the world! During my first summer vacation, I toured the United States.

(below) My job in Nassau was a lot of fun! This picture shows a diorama of the island made by my students. I loved working with children, especially these children.

(above) I taught during the day, but on some evenings and weekends, I looked after these girls while their parents were away on business.

(below) My mother and I have always had a great relationship. She and my father were divorced while I was in Nassau.

(above) This was my house in Nassau, which I shared with three teachers. I could see the beach from my bedroom window.

(below) During summer vacations, I traveled. Here I am in Tucson, Arizona. When I became an author, I wrote several books about the West.

(above) My mother and sister Suzie visited me in Nassau the first Christmas I was there. They loved Nassau, too.

In 1971, after teaching in Nassau for two years, I decided to travel to Europe. The places I wanted to visit most were Hungary and Austria. I hoped to find the Hubers in Vienna, but I didn't have their address. As soon as I saw the Riesenrad ferris wheel, however, I knew my way instantly. I went into some of the

shops in the area where the Hubers had lived and asked if anyone knew them. It took me less than a half hour to find Aunt Burgi. She told me that she and Uncle Hans were divorced, and Elfi, shown above, was married and had a baby named Marion. My friend Bev and I, above left, visited them several times, but then I lost touch with the Hubers again because we still didn't speak the same language.

While writing this book, I realized that the Hubers had played a very important role in my life. They showed me how to trust again. After a month of searching, I located them by phone. That call was a very happy one for us all! Sadly, however, I learned that Uncle Hans is no longer alive.

On the right are Aunt Burgi, Elfi, and Marion today.

194

After visiting the Hubers, I went on to Hungary to see my family and childhood friends. Hungary was still a Communist country then, and I could feel the fear all over again. On my passport it stated that, while I was in Hungary, I would be considered a Hungarian citizen, subject to Hungary's rules. I even had my passport taken away once because I didn't report to the police within 24 hours of being in the country.

It was fun seeing my family and friends in Hungary, but I breathed a sigh of relief when I was back in Austria. This time, I drove across, but the memories of our terrifying crossing in 1956 were still with me. In fact, my border-crossing nightmare haunted me each night that I spent in Hungary!

(below) In Budapest, I am in front of the Parliament Buildings, still run by Soviets and Communists. I wanted to scream out what I thought about them, but I didn't want to be arrested.

(above) Aunt Joli and Uncle Laci, the doctor in my story, showed me around Hungary again. They still live there, but their son Biki, on my left, is now a doctor in Canada.

(below) In Austria, the view at the top of the mountains was always amazing!

(above) I went to Paris often with my friends, the Baudes. Here we are at a New Year's Eve costume party. I was a grape.

I was in Europe for almost two years, traveling and working. For a year, I taught English in Germany, where I learned to speak German. I also spent time in Austria, Spain, and France. By then, I'd been away for almost four years, and it was time to go home.

Unfortunately, I came home at a time when there were more teachers than jobs, so I didn't get a teaching position. But I *did* get a great job marketing the books of several American publishers. My teaching background was very helpful. Part of my job was teaching teachers about social studies and science topics. I loved publishing, but I really wanted to teach. Finally, I had the chance to teach a second-and-third grade class. Before long, however, I got a very important job.

In my new position teaching English as a Second Language, I was in charge of over 100 children from other countries. This was a job I was *meant* to do. Groups of students came to my class at scheduled times during the week. With the help of Barb, my excellent teaching assistant, I created projects for my students that were creative and fun. We made a huge mural on the Arctic, which was almost as long as the hallway of the school, put on plays and fashion shows, and served gourmet multicultural meals.

The part of me that was shoved to the back of the first-grade classroom was still angry and wanted to make sure my immigrant students wouldn't have to feel that kind of rejection! Instead of being invisible, my students became the focus of attention at the school, showing off their intelligence, creativity, and many talents.

That same year, I married Peter Crabtree and became second mother to Caroline, Marc, and Andrea. A year later, we had two babies—one was Samantha, and the other was Crabtree Publishing.

My "princess fantasy," which dates back to my life in Vienna, is evident in our wedding picture.

Peter and I had the same vision for creating books. Our first series was about pioneer life. Peter loves history and art, and pioneer life reminded me of my life with my grandparents in Hungary. We researched the old pictures together and took the photographs ourselves.

Being an author is really fun. It was especially fun at the very beginning, when Peter and I and our children did almost everything ourselves. We typed orders, packed boxes, did mailings, attended conferences—and, of course—wrote the books.

Together with our children, we visited historic places, such as Colonial Williamsburg, to research our many history books. We also traveled to book fairs in the U.S. and Europe. While writing about dolphins and sea turtles, Samantha, below, and I swam with them in Hawaii and in the Caribbean. Peter, Samantha, and I also spent several weeks in the Bahamas writing and taking photographs for *Nicola's Floating Home*, shown left. Nicola now works at the Schönbrunn Zoo in Vienna. I find that coincidence just plain freaky!

My family—Peter, Marc, Caroline, Andrea, and Samantha—on a visit to Nassau. Andrea and Sam work for Crabtree, and Marc is our talented photographer. Caroline is a high-school teacher. We have three grandsons— Sean, Liam, and Charlie.

Since she was young, Sam has modeled in many of our books.

My husband Peter and son Marc traveled together to take pictures for our Lands, Peoples, and Cultures Series. Here, Marc is flying off to take photographs of Brazil for our books.

Left to right; Andrea, me, Sam, Suzanne, Paul, Caroline, and Marc. Suzanne is the mother of our oldest three children. Paul is Caroline's husband. Peter is taking the photo.

I've learned a lot about history, science, and cultures by writing books, but I learned the most about myself writing *this* book. I discovered that the seeds for many of the things I've done in my life were planted during the Revolution or during my stay in Vienna. Until now, I never knew why I did some of these things. For example, I now speak the four languages that Celia spoke— English, German, French, and Hungarian. I've collected hundreds of dolls, not knowing that I was trying to replace the doll I lost at the Austrian border. And, throughout my life, I've mentored many young girls, "paying forward" the kindness the Hubers had shown me. And, I still create my life from my dreams.

I love Hawaii because of its beautiful colors.

Now I know why I collected all those dolls!

Perhaps our three grandsons, Sean, Liam, and Charlie, will be the next Crabtree authors.

Each year, I receive letters from children asking me about my life and how I became an author. I didn't always know that I would be an author, but everything that happened to me led up to it. Life is like a jigsaw puzzle. It is made up of tiny pieces that will one day fit together to reveal the whole picture.

Life is also full of contrasts. There are good times, and there are difficult times. The difficult periods of our lives show us how strong we can be and allow us to discover who we really are. The good times teach us how to love life and feel grateful. No matter what life has in store, we *always* have a choice in how we react to any situation. We can always *choose* to be positive and happy.

Everyone has an amazing story to tell. I hope my story will help you share *your story* with others. Why not start writing it today?

Meeting the Dalai Lama was one of the high points of my life. His Holiness loved our book on Tibet and invited me to meet him. The Dalai Lama was a refugee from Communist China, just as I was a refugee from Communist Hungary.

The Hungarian Revolution

The Hungarian Revolution

In 1956, the people of Hungary joined together to free their country from the Soviet Union, a Communist country. The Soviet Union had turned Hungary into an oppressive Communist nation. Under Communist rule, the country became poverty-stricken, and the people were stripped of their rights and freedoms.

The 1848 Hungarian Revolution

The 1956 Hungarian Revolution had its roots in a struggle for freedom that began over 100 years earlier. On March 15, 1848, the Hungarian people revolted against Austria, which ruled their country. The Hungarians wanted the freedom to govern their own country, without interference from Austria. They wanted their own army, their own independent government, and freedom of the press. They also demanded that all people be treated equally.

Kossuth, the Father of Hungarian Democarcy

One of the most important people in the 1848 Revolution was a man named Lajos Kossuth, known as "the father of Hungarian Democracy." Kossuth wanted Hungary to become a democratic country, in which the people could make all their own political and economic decisions. On March 15, 1848, Kossuth led a group of Hungarians to Austria to place their demands before the Austrian monarchy.

The end of the 1848 Revolution

At first, the Austrians agreed to meet the Hungarian demands. Before long, however, they began to take away some of the freedoms they had granted to Hungary. In December of 1848, Franz Josef was crowned the emperor of Austria. He sent armies to attack Hungary. Army generals such as Jozef Bem, a Polish general, led the Hungarians to victory in many battles. In April of 1849, Hungarians declared that Austria no longer ruled their country. They elected Kossuth as their leader. But by August, 1849, armies from Russia invaded Hungary and helped the Austrians crush the Revolution.

The Dual Monarchy of Austria-Hungary

Between 1849 and 1867, Austria ruled Hungary, but Emperor Franz Josef was very worried that the Hungarians might revolt again. He decided on a compromise with Hungary. A compromise is an agreement in which both sides accept less than what they originally wanted. In 1867, Hungary agreed to Franz Josef's compromise and became part of the Dual Monarchy of Austria-Hungary. Under the Dual Monarchy, the Austrian emperor also became the king of Hungary. He ruled both countries, but each country had its own government. In the early 1900s, Austria-Hungary became prosperous. Hungary provided almost half of the empire's agricultural needs. At the same time, industry was also growing throughout the country. Many people moved to the cities to work in factories. More people than ever before had the opportunity to receive a good education.

The Communist takeover

During World War Two, Hungary fought on the side of Germany, which lost the war. In 1945, at the end of the war, Hungary became occupied by the Soviet Union. An occupied country is controlled by another country's military. Soviet troops committed terrible crimes against the Hungarians. Thousands of Hungarians were sent to work camps in Siberia, a cold, remote part of the Soviet Union. Many did not survive the harsh conditions at these camps.

A Soviet satellite

The Soviet Union was determined to make Hungary a Soviet satellite nation. A satellite nation is a country that is controlled by another country. The Soviets put Communists in charge of Hungary's police forces, industry, transportation, and agriculture. People who opposed the Communist party were arrested and put in jail. By 1949, the Communist party, led by Mátyás Rákosi, had gained complete control of the Hungarian government. Rákosi wanted to mold Hungary into a copy of the Soviet Union. Hungarians were treated like slaves. They decided to fight for their freedom. This fight was called the Hungarian Revolution. The Revolution lasted from October 23 to November 4, 1956.

Seeds planted in Szeged

One of the first steps toward the Revolution was taken by a huge group of university students in Szeged, a city in the south of Hungary (see map on page 12). Under Communism, all university students had to belong to a Communist group called the Union of Working Youth. On October 16, 1956, the students in Szeged quit this group and formed their own group, called Mefész. In Mefész, the students elected their own leaders and made up their own rules. They had never had such freedom before! Within a week, the students sent delegates to Budapest and to other cities in Hungary. Soon, students all over the country had joined Mefész.

Demanding change

On October 22nd, students in Budapest gathered at the Technical University to support an uprising by workers in Poland. Although the Polish Uprising was crushed quickly by the Polish secret police, it made the Hungarian students think about making changes in Hungary! The students drew up a list of 16 demands.

The students' demands

The students' demands included that Soviet troops leave Hungary, that the ÁVH secret police be dissolved, that the government allow more than one political party to exist, and that free elections be held. They wanted the press—and all Hungarians—to be allowed to express their opinions freely. They demanded that everyone have the right to get an education. They wanted Hungary to be equal to the Soviet Union. They demanded that Hungarians be free to practice their traditions and to celebrate holidays, especially March 15th, which commemorated Hungary's brave struggle for freedom in 1848. Celebrating this day was forbidden!

Imre Nagy

The students also wanted Imre Nagy to be prime minister again. He had been the prime minister of Hungary from 1953 to 1955. Although Nagy was a Communist, he believed that people deserved certain rights and freedoms. As a leader, Nagy had made important changes in Hungary. He freed many Hungarians who had been wrongfully jailed. He also placed controls on the ÁVH and allowed some farmers to own land. In 1955, however, Nagy was no longer leading the country, and these rights were taken away. The Hungarian people believed that if Nagy was made prime minister again, he would restore these freedoms.

October 23rd—The Uprising

On October 23rd, a huge group of students led a protest through the streets of Budapest. Some marched to the statue of Jozef Bem to show their support for the Polish workers, whose uprising had been crushed. Some marched to the Parliament Buildings. When the Communists at the Parliament Buildings saw the huge crowd outside, they turned off all the lights. The crowd then headed to the radio station, Radio Budapest, to join another huge crowd that had assembled there. By then, over 200,000 people had gathered there! They wanted the students' demands to be read over the radio, and they shouted for the Soviet troops to go home. Even though people were speaking their minds, they behaved peacefully. But the ÁVH wanted them silenced and became angry. The peaceful protest soon turned violent.

(left) People gathered at the statue of Polish General Bem.

(below) Later that evening, a huge crowd assembled at the Parliament Buildings. They demanded to see Imre Nagy. The Communists turned off all the lights.

The fighting begins

Members of the ÁVH fired bullets into the crowd, killing several people. The students were very angry that the ÁVOs had killed peaceful protesters. They ran through the streets of Budapest, turning over police cars. People gathered guns and handed them out among the crowd. Some of the protesters marched to a 60-foot (18-m) tall statue of Joseph Stalin, a former Soviet leader, and pulled it down (see photo on page 59). They dragged the broken pieces of the statue through the streets. The Hungarian Uprising was now officially the Hungarian Revolution.

October 24th—Imre Nagy becomes leader

On October 24th, thousands of other Hungarians joined the fight. People armed themselves with guns and Molotov cocktails, or homemade bombs. As the fighting continued in the streets of Budapest, Imre Nagy was once again made the leader of Hungary.

Help from the army

Soviet military forces had been stationed in the countryside of Hungary since the end of World War Two. When the Revolution began, these forces moved into Budapest to try to silence the Hungarian people. The Communist government also called on the Hungarian army for help. Many of the soldiers wanted to support their own people, however. Under the direction of Pál Maléter, a commander of the Hungarian army, the soldiers fought alongside the freedom fighters and provided them with Soviet weapons.

(*above*) *Young children climbed on the tanks. They fought bravely in the streets.*
(*below*) *The Hungarian army joined in the fight against the Soviets.*

October 25th—More violence

On October 25th, protesters once again gathered at the Parliament Buildings, shown below, and demanded to see Imre Nagy. ÁVOs were lined up on the roofs of the buildings with machine guns. They soon fired into the crowd, killing dozens of people.

October 26th—Massacre in Mosonmagyaróvár

By October 26th, the Revolution had spread to the countryside. A crowd of peaceful protesters in Mosonmagyaróvár, made up mainly of students and factory workers, marched through the town, tearing down Soviet symbols, such as red stars. Eventually, they headed to the town's ÁVH barracks to tell the ÁVOs to join them or leave the city. At the barracks, the ÁVOs fired on the crowd. More than 100 men, women, and children were killed, and hundreds more were wounded. When people in Budapest heard about the terrible massacre, they hunted down ÁVOs all over Budapest and killed them without mercy.

October 28th to 30th—A promise of hope

On October 28th, Imre Nagy spoke over the radio to let people know that the Soviet troops were leaving Budapest. He promised that Hungary would no longer have a secret police force and that people would be allowed to own property. Nagy then asked Hungarians to put down their guns. Some Hungarians continued to fight, however. On October 30th, the rebels took over an ÁVH prison outside Budapest. They freed many political prisoners, including Cardinal József Mindszenty, the head of the Roman Catholic Church in Hungary. He had been jailed by the Communists eight years earlier for opposing Communism. Cardinal Mindszenty's release was celebrated by Hungarians.

October 31st to November 3rd—Days of peace

By October 31st, people could see that Soviet troops were pulling out of Budapest. For the first time, they felt hopeful that their struggle had been worth it. Free press was established all over the country, and Soviet symbols were pulled down. Imre Nagy abolished the ÁVH. Hungarians celebrated and began to rebuild their nation. On November 1st, Nagy declared Hungary to be an independent country, in the hope that Western countries such as Britain and the United States would come to its aid.

November 4th—The Soviets return

Unfortunately, the Soviet Union had already planned another attack. A huge Soviet army of over 250,000 men swept into Hungary. On November 4th, the army attacked Budapest and crushed the Hungarian Revolution. At the same time, the Suez War broke out in Egypt. France, the United Kingdom, and Israel attacked Egypt, and the Soviet Union threatened to fight on Egypt's side. Some of the Soviet soldiers who were fighting in Hungary actually believed they were at the Suez Canal in Egypt!

The end of the Revolution

The Hungarian Revolution lasted only a few weeks. In that time, thousands of Hungarians and Soviet troops were killed, and many were injured. Western nations spoke out against the cruelty of the Soviet Union, but they did nothing to help. Hungary sent distress signals to the world. People at Radio Free Europe heard the signals and assured Hungary that the U.S. was sending troops to help. They urged the Hungarians to keep fighting.

No help for Hungary

Unfortunately, the United States never intended to help. Americans were afraid that World War Three might break out if the U.S. got involved in the Hungarian Revolution. The United Nations did not help Hungary, either, because it was trying to make peace in Egypt. Hungary was abandoned by the world! Radio Free Europe's message caused hundreds more Hungarians to die fighting a losing battle. The Revolution soon ended, and 200,000 Hungarians fled the country. They became refugees in neighboring countries such as Austria and Yugoslavia. In Hungary, hundreds of people were executed, including Imre Nagy and Pál Maléter.

A tear in the curtain

In spite of its tragic ending, the Revolution proved that Hungarians were willing to risk their lives for freedom. The Revolution created a tear in the Iron Curtain, which allowed people in many other Soviet countries to gain their freedom in the years that followed. In 1989, Hungary became the first nation under Soviet control to gain a democratic government. This government allowed people from other Communist countries to cross Hungary's borders into Austria and Yugoslavia. By 1990, Soviet countries such as Czechoslovakia, Hungary, Poland, Romania, Bulgaria, and East Germany had abandoned their Communist governments. In East Germany, the Berlin Wall was taken down, and, by 1991, the Soviet Union was officially finished. The people of Eastern Europe were finally free!

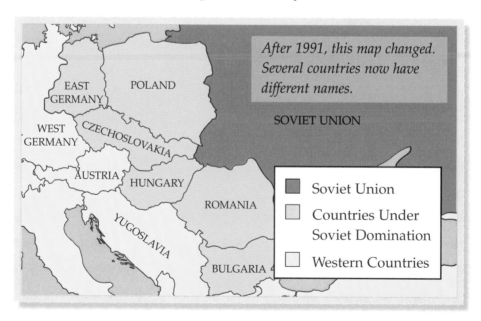

After 1991, this map changed. Several countries now have different names.

During the Revolution, thousands of people fought bravely, and many were killed. Although Budapest was badly damaged, the Revolution was worth the struggle, as it started the downfall of the Soviet Union.

Never forget!

Many people still live without human rights today, including those who live in existing Communist countries. Human rights are basic freedoms that allow people to live with dignity. All people deserve the right to speak their minds without fear. They deserve to choose where they will live and to elect governments for their countries. All people deserve to be educated, to be free to practice their religions, and to be proud of their cultures. We must never forget that some people had to fight for these human rights. If we forget about important historic events such as the Hungarian Revolution, we take these rights for granted. We must never forget!

Glossary

anthem A song declaring loyalty to a country

antibiotic A substance that kills bacteria in the body

ÁVH The organization of secret police in Hungary

ÁVO An ÁVH officer

barracks Buildings that house military personnel

betrayal An act of being disloyal or harmful

Catholic Belonging to the Roman Catholic Church

censor To remove parts of radio transmissions or publications that are considered unacceptable

coat of arms A design on a shield that represents a family, country, or people

Communism A political system in which everything is owned and directed by the government

courtyard An area surrounded by buildings

cuisine High-quality cooking

curfew A time after which people are not allowed outdoors

currency A system of money

defect To abandon a country for political or moral reasons

demonstration A public display for or against an issue or cause

descendant Someone related to someone from the past

dismantle To take something apart so it no longer works

dual monarchy Two kingdoms ruled by one ruler

embassy A building in one country that represents another country and can be a safe haven

empower To give power or authority to someone

execute To put someone to death

flare A device used to cause a sudden blaze of light in the sky

freedom fighter Someone who participates in an armed revolt against a government

gangway A walkway into a ship

goulash A Hungarian meat stew

hand grenade A small bomb designed to be thrown by hand

headquarters The main offices of an organization

human rights The rights, such as freedom, considered by most societies to belong to everyone

immigration The act of entering a new country to live there

informant Someone who gives information that causes problems for another

Iron Curtain The armed border that blocked the free exchange of ideas between Communist countries and Western countries

journalist Someone who works as a writer or an editor for radio, TV, or a newspaper or magazine

Magyar Hungarian

mass A Catholic Church service

mass funeral The burial of a large group of people

massacre The killing of a large number of people

media Various means of communication

Molotov cocktail A homemade bomb made by pouring gasoline into a bottle and lighting a wick

occupation The invasion and control of a country

ocean liner A passenger ship

omen A sign of things to come

paprika A mild red pepper spice

pew A bench in a church

police state A country that uses secret police to enforce control

political prisoner Someone who is imprisoned for political reasons

political science The study of political systems or governments

propaganda Information spread by a government to support or spread its causes or ideas

protester Someone who expresses strong disapproval of something

refugee Someone who leaves a country at war to seek safety

reign of terror A time when a government frightens people

revolution An uprising against a government

rheumatic fever A disease causing pain, swelling, and a high fever

scarlet fever A disease that causes fever and a rash

SOS Distress radio signals

Soviet Relating to the former Soviet Union or its people

traitor A person who betrays his or her country

treason The betrayal of one's own country

United Nations An organization of countries formed in 1945 to promote peace, security, and international cooperation

victim A person who feels helpless in the face of misfortune

visa Official papers authorizing travel to a country

West Non-communist countries in Europe and North and South America

Index

Bibliography and Websites

Books:

Grove, Andrew S. *Swimming Across*. New York: Warner Books, 2001.

Hebert, Charles; Norm Longley; and Dan Richardson. *The Rough Guide to Hungary*. New York: Rough Guides Ltd, 2005.

Hill, Raymond. *Nations in Transition: Hungary*. New York: Facts on File, Inc., 1997.

Kopacsi, Sandor. *"In the Name of the Working Class."* Toronto: Lester & Orpen Denny's Ltd., 1979.

Kosary, Dominic G.; Steven Bela Vardy; and the Danubian Research Center. *History of the Hungarian Nation*. Florida: Danubian Press Inc., 1969.

Macartney, C.A. *Hungary: A Short History*. Edinburgh: Edinburgh University Press, 1962.

Marton, Endre. *The Forbidden Sky: Inside the Hungarian Revolution*. Boston: Little, Brown & Company, 1971.

McNair-Wilson, Diana. *Hungary*. London: B.T. Batsford Ltd., 1976.

Pryce-Jones, David. *The Hungarian Revolution*. New York: Horizon Press, 1970.

Websites:

Kalman, Bobbie. Refugee Child. http://bobbiekalmanrefugeechild.com

The American Hungarian Federation.
http://www.americanhungarianfederation.org/about.htm
http://www.americanhungarianfederation.org/featured.htm
http://www.hungary1956.com/

Blunden, Andy. "The Hungarian Uprising, 1956." Greenfield History Site.
http://www.johndclare.net/cold_war14_hungary_1956.htm

Corvinus Library: Hungarian History.
http://www.hungarianhistory.com/lib/revol.htm

Gati Productions. "1956 Hungarian Revolution: A Brief Annotated Photo Chronology." Starting Over in America.
http://fog.ccsf.cc.ca.us/~sgati/gatiproductions/starting_over/revolution.htm

"History of the 1956 Hungarian Revolution." The Institute for the History of the 1956 Hungarian Revolution.
http://www.rev.hu/history_of_56/naviga/index.htm

Hungarian American Coalition, The. http://www.hhrf.org/hac/
http://www.freedomfighter56.com/en_history.html

Johnson, Major Charles Christopher. "Revolt Revisited—A Study Of The Hungarian Revolution of October, 1956." GlobalSecurity.org.
http://www.globalsecurity.org/military/library/report/1984/JCC.htm

"Map of Old Vienna." http://www.wien.info/wtv/plan/uebersicht.html

Othfors, Daniel. "Gripsholm/MS Berlin history." The Great Ocean Liners.
http://www.greatoceanliners.net/gripsholm1.html

Pier 21 - Gateway to Canada. http://www.pier21.ca/

Rakoczi Foundation and Multicultural History Society of Ontario. "The Hungarian Exodus." 1956 Memorial.
http://www.1956memorial.com/exhibit.html

Schönbrunn Palace. "Virtual tour (Grand Tour)." Schönbrunn official site.
http://www.schoenbrunn.at/en/site/publicdir/0103020200_101.php#49073

"Universal declaration of human rights." United Nations.
http://www.un.org/Overview/rights.html